Nikon Coolpix p950 Illustrated Guide

A Visual Handbook to p950 Mastery, from Beginner to Pro

By

Herbert Gunta

TABLE OF CONTENTS

INTRODUCTION

With its 83x optical zoom lens, the COOLPIX P950 can cover an amazing variety of focal lengths, from the wide-angle 24 mm equivalent to the super-telephoto 2000 mm equivalent (with Dynamic Fine Zoom activated, the lens can zoom up to 166x). The COOLPIX P950 is a tiny digital camera that replaces the COOLPIX P900; it has more user-friendly features and better video recording capabilities than its predecessor.

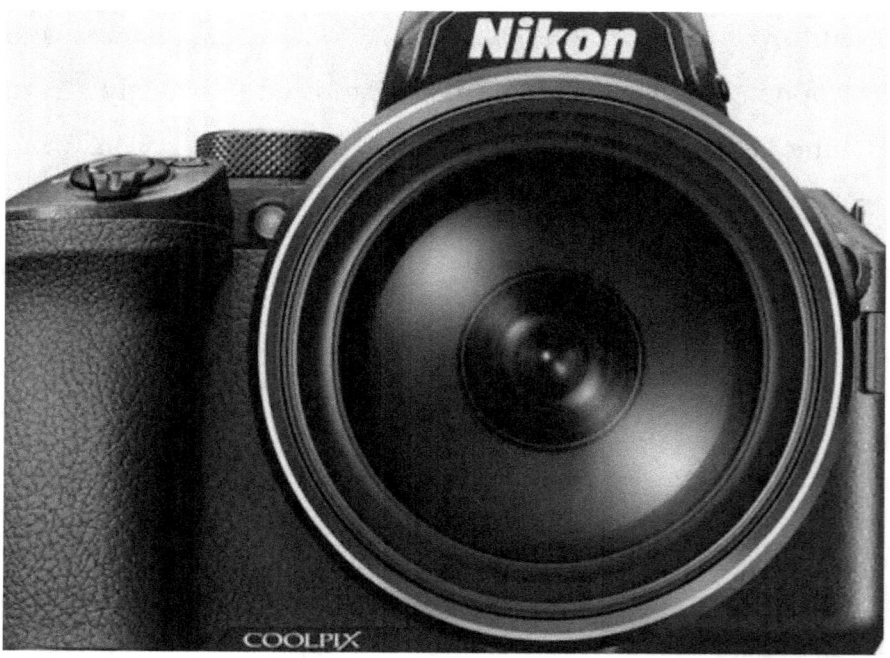

With a rear end illumination CMOS image sensor, a quick and highly accurate EXPEED image-processing engine, and a Super ED (Extra-low Dispersion) lens element, the camera provides an effective pixel count of 16.0. This results in excellent image quality across the zoom range. Its Dual Detect Optical VR function, which is also the most potent vibration reduction feature in the history of Nikon small digital cameras, offers more precise compensation with image-stabilization capabilities, which is comparable to a 5.5-stop improvement in shutter speed. This makes hand-held photography possible, even at super-telephoto zoom settings, producing crisp, clear photographs. Furthermore, since the COOLPIX P900, movie recording features have advanced significantly. The COOLPIX P950 is capable of recording in 4K UHD/30p and Movie Manual mode, which lets the user adjust exposure levels. It also has a function that lets you alter the zoom speed while you are filming.

The ergonomics and functionality of the COOLPIX P950 have been enhanced by the addition of an approximately 2359k-dot OLED electronic viewfinder, a focus-mode selector that allows for quick switching between focus modes, and a side dial that can be used for both manual and autofocus focusing (MF and AF). Furthermore, the COOLPIX P950 has an accessory shoe that can accommodate a range of accessories. One such attachment is the DF-M1 Dot Sight, which is an optional device that enables users to create images with telephoto and super-telephoto photography of distant targets, such birds and celestial bodies.

With the COOLPIX P950 digital camera, you can fully enjoy all forms of photography, from landscapes and animals to astronomy and birds.

Other Specifications of the Camera;

1. **Super-telephoto shooting at your fingertips with a magnification of 2,000 mm:** The 83x optical zoom NIKKOR lens that comes with the COOLPIX P950 spans the focal length range of 24 mm to 2000 mm, super telephoto to wide angle. Sharp and crisp resolution is ensured throughout the full zoom range thanks to lens optics that have one Super ED and five ED lens elements incorporated. This effectively compensates for the chromatic aberration that often arises with super-telephoto photography. Furthermore, shooting at the equivalent of around 4000 mm is feasible when Dynamic Fine Zoom is used. The most potent vibration reduction feature in the history of Nikon small digital cameras is its Dual Detect Optical VR function, which provides picture stabilization comparable to a 5.5-stop shutter speed improvement. This makes it possible to take quick, handheld photos in the field—even at super-telephoto zoom angles—in situations where using a tripod would be difficult or cumbersome. To enable users to effectively capture every ideal moment as it happens, AF performance at telephoto locations has been improved, and the buffer has been enlarged for greater continuous shooting performance.

2. **Capturing movies in 4K UHD/30p with more realism:** It is possible to record 4K UHD/30p high definition video with the COOLPIX P950. It is capable of capturing very dramatic and forceful films at super-telephoto 2000 mm equivalent. Moreover, still photographs of pivotal events may be

8

preserved by saving movie frames captured in 4K UHD format.

3. **Ability to modify the Zoom speed when capturing a movie:** The camera lens zoom rates may be adjusted to High-speed movie zoom, Mid-speed movie zoom, or Low-speed movie zoom when the side zoom control is used for movie recording. By selecting a slower zoom speed to create a cinematic impression, for example, users may capture more imaginative and artistic videos. Aperture adjustments made when zooming throughout a video are also seamless and hardly flicker during natural exposure changes.

4. **The Camera supports the unique NRW (RAW) file format:** The COOLPIX P950 allows NRW (RAW) file recording of picture data that is read from the image sensor while taking still photos. These files may be edited and retouched using Nikon's RAW image processing software, Capture NX-D or ViewNX-i, to get the desired effects without sacrificing picture quality.

5. **Excellent performance that facilitates comfortable shooting:** The COOLPIX P950 has a 3.2-inch vari-angle display with a broad viewing angle and an approximately 2359k-dot OLED electronic viewfinder with an eye sensor. Additionally, it has a side dial that allows the user to change the focus in MF mode or carry out an assigned function in AF mode without diverting their attention from the viewfinder. The COOLPIX P950 has additional features that allow for more flexible reaction to shooting settings, sceneries, or

subjects. These controls include an AE-L/AF-L button for locking exposure and/or focus, and a focus-mode selector for instantaneous switching between AF (autofocus) and MF (manual focus) modes.

6. **The Camera supports a wider range of visual expression**: An accessory shoe and an accessory terminal that may accommodate a large number of accessories are included with the COOLPIX P950. Users can enjoy an operational experience similar to that of digital SLR cameras with accessories like a dot sight, which may help with super-telephoto photography of small or distant subjects like birds and celestial bodies; speedlights, which allow for flexible lighting control; and microphones, which allow for realistic recording of wild animal calls, concerts, and other events.

7. It has Moon and Bird-watching modes that are easily accessible using the mode dial.

8. For taking long-exposure photos, the Camera offers choices for both bulb and time exposure.

9. The camera supports SnapBridge, which allows for automated picture transfers to a smart device and remote camera control from a smart device.

10. The camera has a creative mode that makes it easy to get the perfect visual expression.

FIRST-TIME CAMERA CONFIGURATION

Unboxing the Camera

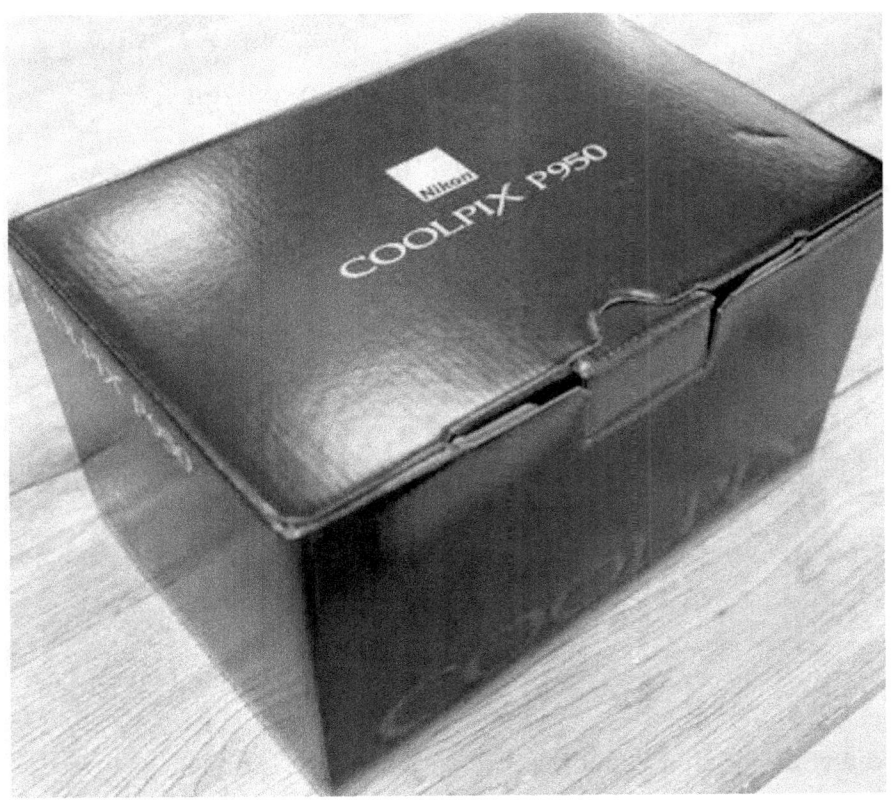

When you unbox the Nikon Coolpix 950, you should find the following alongside the Camera; The Nikon lithium-ion battery, battery terminal cover, charging adapter, neck harness, USB cable, lens covering, lens shield, and a concise "Quick Start Guide" pamphlet. A registration card and a safety notice should also be included. The HDMI cable required to connect the camera to a television or an external monitor is not included in

11

the box, nor is the complete instruction manual or software in the disc you will find inside the box. So, if you want the complete PDF version of the Nikon reference manual, you can obtain it from the website http://nikonimglib.com/manual/. Additionally, the manual is available online at https://onlinemanual.nikonimglib.com/p950/en.

- **Insertion and Charging of the Battery**

The EN-EL20a is the Nikon battery recommended for the Coolpix P950. To charge the battery, connect the camera to an AC receptacle using the included charger. You can also connect the camera to a USB interface on a computer or other device using the USB cable that is included with the camera. Also note, the charging process does not require the removal of the battery from the camera. Hence, the camera can be charged by simply connecting it to an external power source. However, the camera cannot be used while the battery is being charged.

To charge the camera's battery, open the cover at the bottom of the camera and thereafter insert the battery. Note, there is only one direction through which the battery can be inserted into the camera. So you should observe the four gold-colored contacts located along one edge of the battery and position them adjacent to the camera's exterior edge, as the battery is inserted into the compartment.

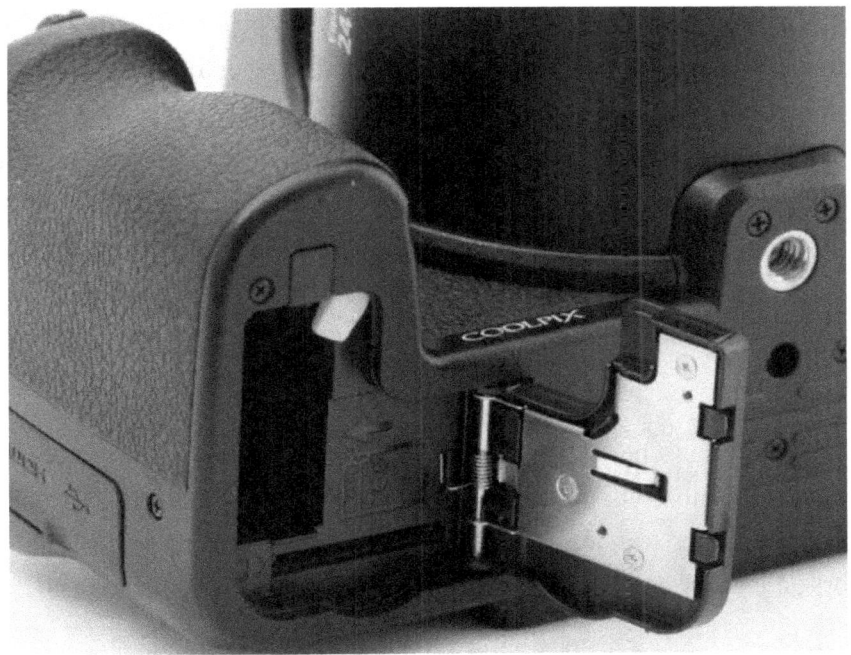

Do not force the battery into the compartment if it will not fit completely; instead, verify its orientation and ensure that it is being inserted in the proper manner. To make sure the battery is completely inserted into its designated slot, push the orange plastic retaining latch to one side, so that the battery will go down into its compartment. Once the battery is secured in position, the latch will anchor the battery.

After inserting the battery into the camera, connect the USB cable by inserting the tiny end into the receptacle located beneath the cover that bears the HDMI and USB symbols on the right side of the camera. Connect the charging adapter that is included with the camera to the other end of the USB cable.

After that, connect the charging adapter to a surge protector or standard electrical receptacle. As the battery charges, the power switch on top of the camera will be accompanied by a green light that blinks approximately twice per second. Once the light turns off, the battery will be completely charged. For a completely dead battery to fully charge, it takes approximately three hours to. This is because the battery requires a considerable amount of time to completely charge; therefore, it is advisable to acquire additional batteries and an external charger.

Note: You can charge the camera's battery through a computer and this is accessible via the camera's menu options, which enables users to connect their device through a USB cable, to a compatible USB port on a computer, in order to charge the camera's battery.

How to Insert the Memory Card

The Coolpix P950 does not include a memory card when you first buy it. When the camera is powered on without a memory card inserted, the message "No card present" will appear in the center of the screen. If you disregard this notification and proceed with the shutter button to capture an image using the default configuration, no action will be taken; the camera will not permit shutter operation in the absence of a memory card. To enable the capture of images without a memory card, you have to modify the default Camera Settings by selecting the Slot Empty Release Lock option from the Setup menu. By selecting Enable Release rather than Release Locked from that menu, the shutter will function, enabling you to capture a limited number of still images for later playback. However, "Demo Mode" will be displayed on each of those images. Note: The camera will delete prior demo images if you capture more than a few. Therefore, an appropriate memory card must be inserted in order to utilize the camera effectively.

Note: SD cards, which are utilized by the P950, are approximately the size of a postage stamp. They are available in different varieties.

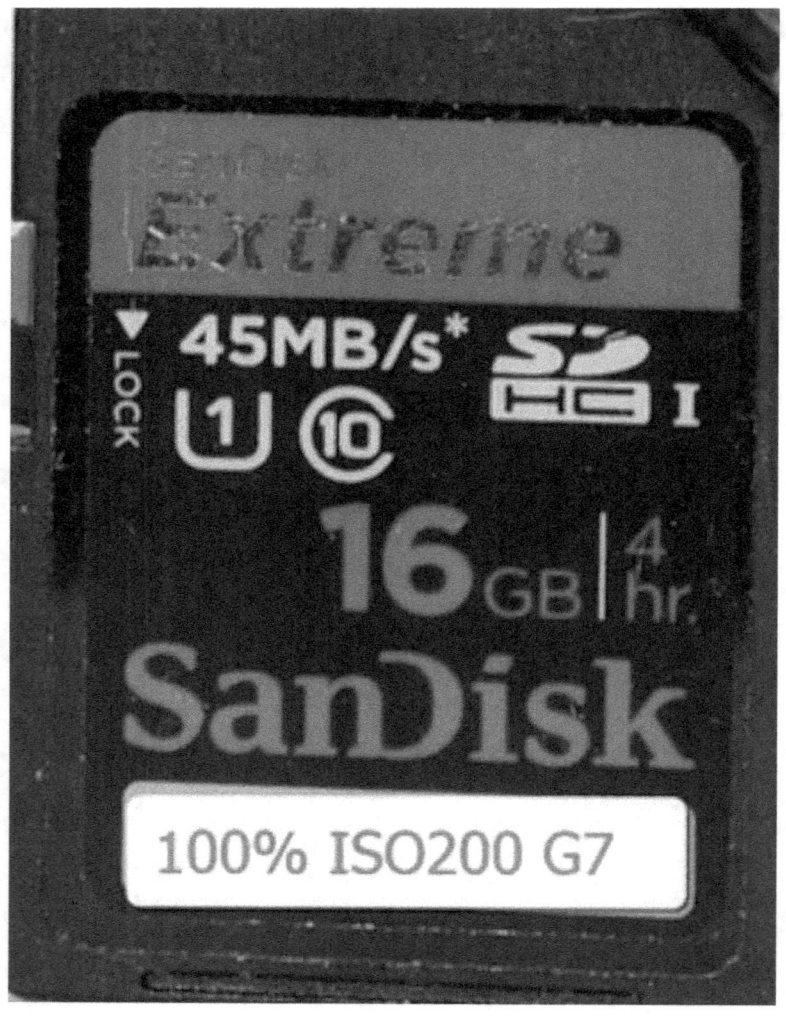

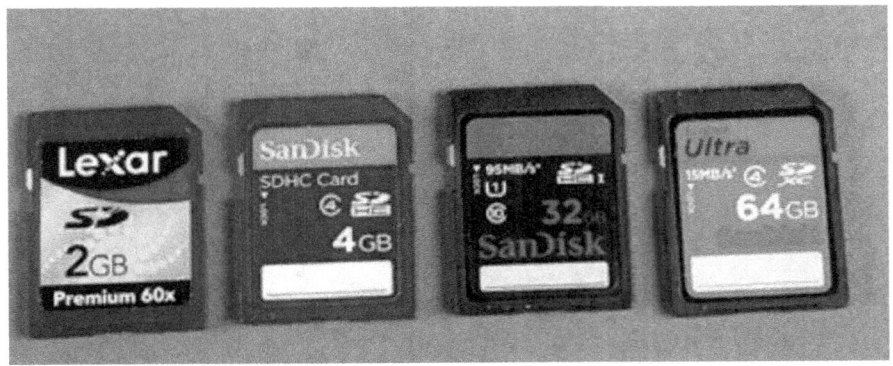

The SD cards which are also called Standard Cards, are available in capacities ranging from 8 MB to 2 GB. SDHC cards are the next highest capacity cards and range in size from 4 GB to 32 GB. Moreso, there is also a larger memory card called the SDXC (for extended capacity) model, which is available in the following capacities: 48 GB, 64 GB, 128 GB, 256 GB, 512 GB, and 1 TB (terabyte); this variant of the card has a maximum capacity of 2 TB. SDXC cards exhibit superior transmission rates in comparison to smaller-capacity cards.

Additionally, the P950 is compatible with micro-SD cards, which are smaller storage media, and are often utilized by smartphones and other compact devices. These cards function identically to SD cards; however, an adapter that is the size of an SD card is required to insert this micro-SD card into the Coolpix P950 camera.

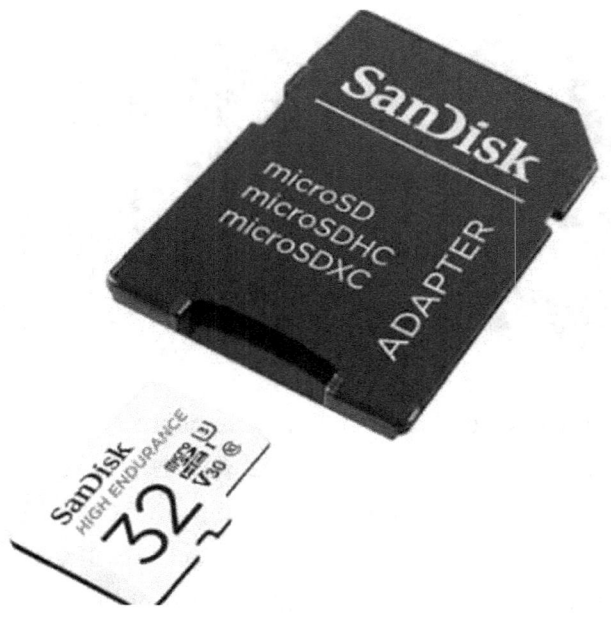

Going further, the memory card type and size you employ are determined by your specific requirements and objectives. Consider purchasing a memory card with a sizable storage capacity if you intend to capture a substantial amount of high-definition (HD), 4K, or still images. When calculating the number of images or videos that can be stored on a specific memory card size, several factors must be considered, including the aspect ratio (16:9, 4:3, 3:2, or 1:1), image size, and quality.

The following are several illustrations of the approximate number of images that can be stored on a 32 GB SDHC card: With the Raw+Fine image quality setting enabled, a 32 GB card has the capacity to store approximately 900 images. The card has the capacity to store approximately 3700 still photographs at its maximum resolution of 4608 x 3456 pixels and with Fine quality. At the minimum resolution of 3264 x 2448 pixels and with Fine quality, the card can accommodate around 6800 images. With Fine quality and reduced image dimensions (1660 x 1200 pixels), the card can store over 10,000 images. It should be noted that the quantity of images that can be stored is subject to variation depending on aspect ratio and image subject matter. Therefore, the figures provided are approximations.

Another factor to take into account is the card's quickness. If you frequently shoot with continuous shooting mode (bursts) or intend to record high-quality video, you should invest in a card with a Class 6 or higher speed rating. But a card with a UHS Speed Class 3 rating is required if you intend to record video at the highest definition preset for 4K (ultra-HD); otherwise, the camera might fail to record the video successfully.

After selecting your memory card, slide it into the card slot until it clicks, with the label facing the rear of the camera. The Card Slot is to be accessed through the same door located on the bottom of the camera, which conceals the battery compartment. After inserting the card until it becomes secure in its slot, close the compartment door and reposition the latch to its locking position. To bring out the card from its slot, keep pressing the card downwards until it shoots outward, enabling you to take it.

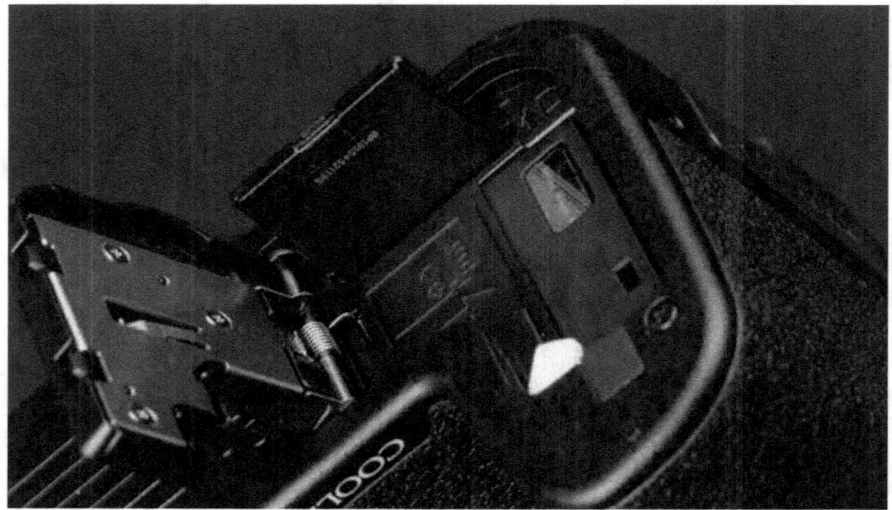

Note; When writing image data to the memory card, the camera illuminates numbers in the lower right angle of the camera display, to signify the number of remaining images or minutes of video. This feature is applicable when using the P950 to capture continuous images. It is also advisable not to turn off the camera or otherwise interfere with its operation when the display is blinking; also do not remove the battery or disconnect an AC power adapter when the display is flashing. But wait until the card has fully completed its recording procedure before doing anything else.

EXTERNAL BUTTONS AND CONTROLS ON THE CAMERA

It is essential to begin by introducing the primary controls so that you can determine which button or dial corresponds to which function or setting.

Control and Button on the Camera's Top

Several important controls and dials are located atop the camera. The critical controls have been explained in the list below:

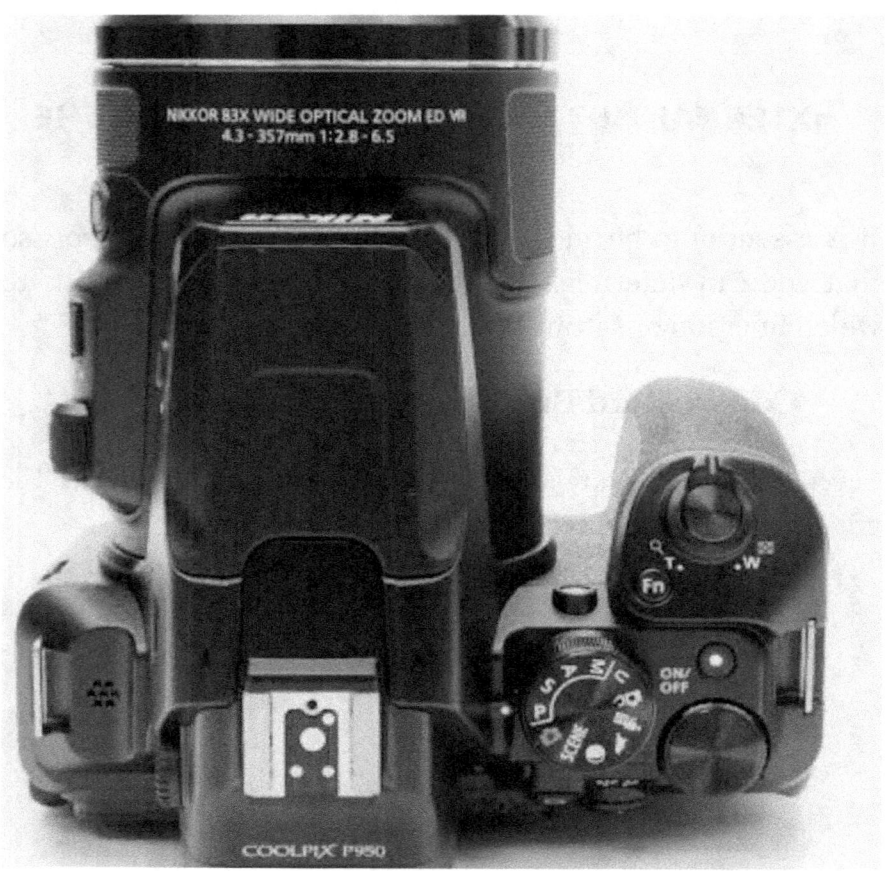

1. The Mode Dial: This is utilized to determine the mode of photography for still images. When adjusting this dial, ensure the green camera icon is positioned adjacent to the white selection marker for basic shooting, enabling the camera to make the majority of decisions.

2. The Shutter Release Button: To capture an image, utilize the Shutter Release Button; hold it halfway down to secure focus and exposure, and fully down to capture a photograph. In

Movie Manual mode, this button initiates and terminates the recording of a movie.

3. The Zoom Lever: This is located adjacent to the shutter release button. In shooting mode, it controls the lens's focal length, ranging from wide-angle to telephoto. In playback mode, it is employed to display index screens or enlarge images.

4. The Function Button: This is a customizable control that grants quick access to a specific menu option as desired.

5. The Power Switch: This is responsible for activating and deactivating the camera.

6. The Microphone: This is utilized to capture audio during film recording.

7. The Command Dial: Although situated atop the camera, the Command Dial is easiest to access by utilizing the forefinger from the rear of the device.

8. The Single Speaker: Located in the upper left corner of the camera, this component produces audio for videos and operational audios.

9. The Accessory Shoe: Accessories like a dot sight, an external flash device, or a microphone can be attached to the camera via the Accessory Shoe.

Controls and Buttons on the Back of the Camera

The back controls of the camera are described in the following list:

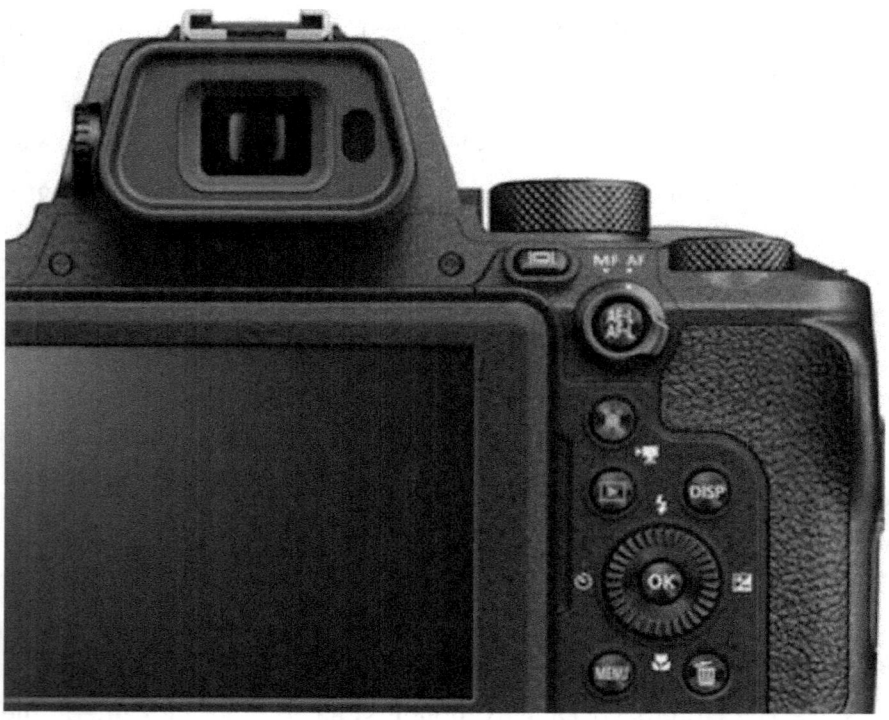

1. The Viewfinder: is the aperture through which one can take photos and review captured images when the LCD screen is folded in against the camera and when the viewfinder has been activated via the eye sensor or the monitor button.

2. The Eye Sensor: Located to the right of the viewfinder window, the Eye Sensor detects the user's head in close proximity to the viewfinder and transitions the screen from the LCD to the viewfinder. Nevertheless, this is modifiable via the EVF Auto Toggle option located in the Setup menu options.

3. The Monitor Button: Utilizing the monitor button toggles the display between the LCD screen and the viewfinder.

4. The Display Button: This button selects displays containing information regarding the shooting environment and the captured images during the recording and playback processes, respectively.

5. The Red Movie Button: This button initiates and terminates a video sequence recording process.

6. The Delete Button: This is also referred to as the Trash button, is utilized to delete previously captured images.

7. The Command Dial: This is situated atop the camera, although it is most conveniently accessed from the rear. It enables the selection of parameters including shutter speed and flexible program, in addition to performing various auxiliary operations in playback and shooting modes.

8. The AE-L/AF-L Button: Exposure, focus, or both may be locked with the AE-L/AF-L button, however, there has to be a configuration of the AE/AF Lock button in the Setup menu.

9. The Focus Mode Selector: This button is positioned in close proximity to the AE-L/AF-L button, and it enables you to toggle the camera between manual and autofocus modes.

10. The Playback Button: This button enables the user to watch recorded images and videos by putting the camera into playback mode.

11. The Menu Button: This button activates the camera's Menu Screens options, which contain a variety of shooting and other value settings, including those for shooting features and control functions.

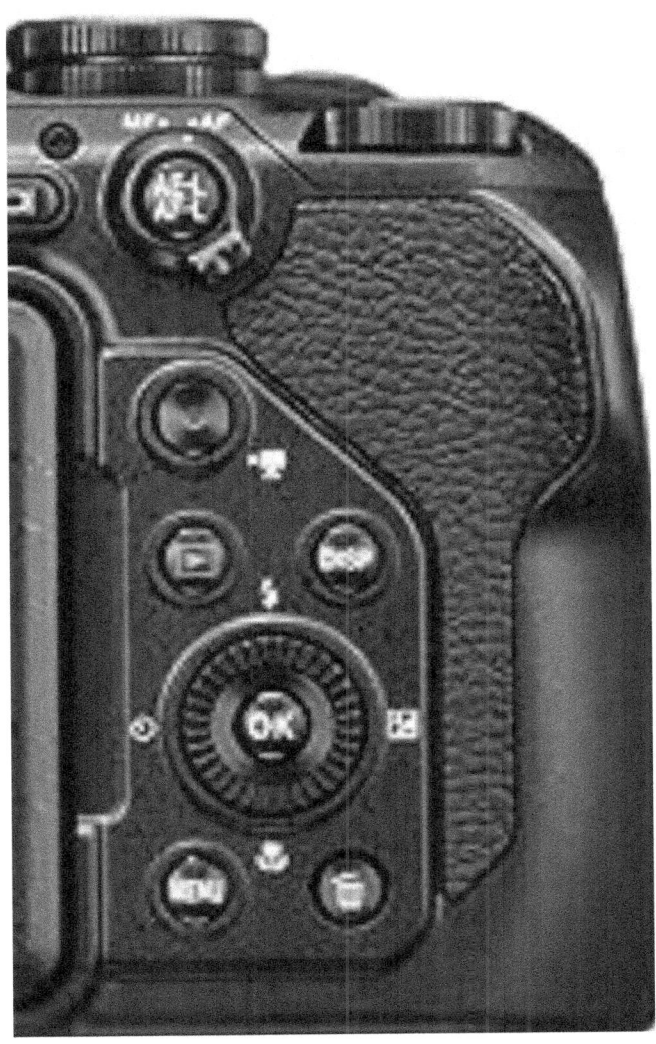

12. The Multi Selector Dial: This dial functions as a wheel that controls aperture and menu screens, as well as screens that

require the user to enter values for a variety of options. You can utilize it to navigate through your captured images and videos during playback mode. Furthermore, when one presses on one of the four edges of the dial, it functions as a button, allowing for the selection of functions such as the self-timer, exposure compensation, flash mode, and focus mode. The corresponding nomenclature of the edges of the Multi Selector Dial are labeled as follows: Up, Down, Left, and Right controls or buttons.

13. The OK Button: This is situated in the dial's center, and serves the purpose of confirming selected options and executing certain secondary operations.

Front and Side Buttons and Controls of the Camera

The important buttons and controls under here have described in the following list:

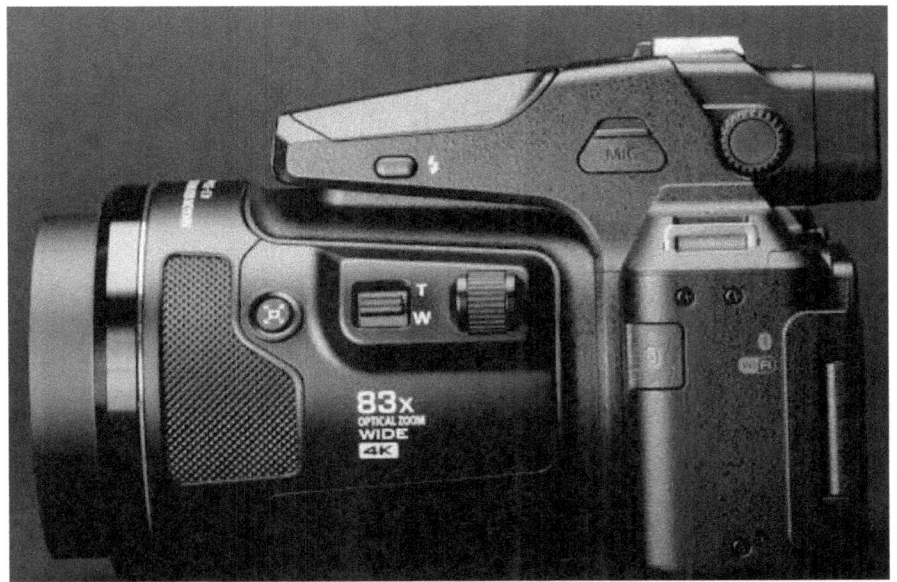

1. The Flash Pop-up Switch: The location of the Flash Pop-up Switch is in the upper left corner of the P950. Its function is to activate the built-in flash unit of the camera, enabling it to discharge when necessary.

2. The Side Zoom Control: With the Side Zoom Control, one can enlarge the lens. The pace at which video is zoomed during recording can be modified by selecting the Assign Side Zoom Control option from the Setup menu.

3. The Snap-back Zoom Button: While holding this button down, it rapidly adjusts the zoom lens to a wider field of view in order to assist in locating distant subjects within the field of view.

4. The Side Dial: Positioned posterior to the side zoom control, this dial is utilized to modify the focus setting in the manual focus mode selector. This dial executes the function designated for it via the Assign Side Dial option on the Setup menu when autofocus is enabled.

5. The Diopter Adjustment Wheel: This control is situated in close proximity to the left side of the viewfinder. It is utilized to fine-tune the viewfinder to the user's vision.

6. The External Microphone Jack: This is utilized to connect an external microphone in place of the built-in microphone, when recording sound for movies.

7. The Accessory Terminal: This terminal facilitates the connection of supplementary remote control devices.

8. The HDMI Port: With an optional HDMI cable, this port is used to connect the camera to an HDTV for the purpose of playing back images and videos. Additionally, it can produce a "clean" HDMI signal for external video recording.

9. The USB Port: This port facilitates the connection between the camera and a computer or charger/power adapter by, through the cable that is included in the camera package.

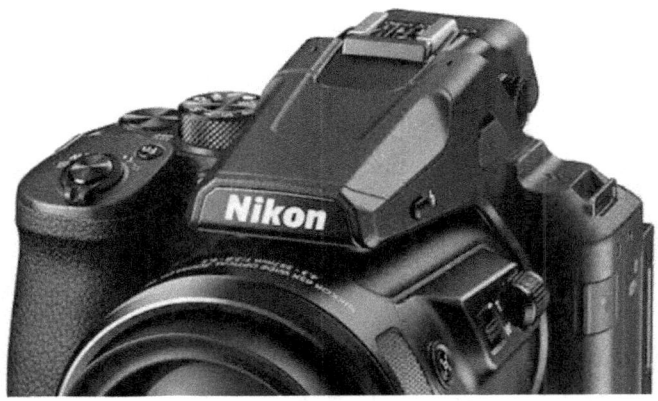

10. Red-eye Reduction/AF Assist/Self-timer illumination: This lamp illuminates to assist the camera in utilizing its autofocus technology in low-light conditions and to indicate that the self-timer is operating. Furthermore, in modes that employ Red-eye Reduction, this brilliant illumination comes on prior to the discharge of the flash, in order to constrict the pupils of a subject's eyes, thereby preventing the flash from reflecting off the retinas and causing the undesirable "red-eye" effect.

11. The Lens: This zoom lens has an optical magnification range and a focal length lens, which is between 24mm and 2000mm. The aperture adjustments of the lens span the range of f/2.8 to f/8.0.

Controls and Buttons Located at the Bottom of the Camera

The camera features three primary controls located at the bottom:

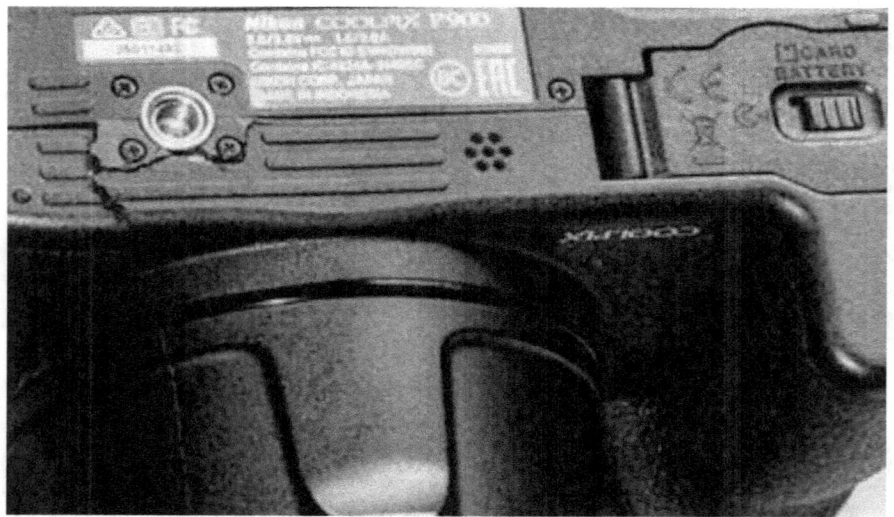

1. The Tripod Socket: This enables a standard fastener to be used to mount the camera to a tripod.

2. The Latch Door: This provides access to the compartment containing the memory card and battery. Note, since the distance between the tripod adapter and the battery/memory card compartment is far, it is possible to access the battery and memory card while the camera is mounted on a tripod.

3. AC Adapter: When installing the optional AC adapter into the camera, a flap along the outer edge of the battery compartment door must be opened to allow the door to close with the cord passing through the channel which the flap inhabits.

BASIC CAMERA OPERATIONS AND SETTINGS

After the Coolpix P950 has been configured with the accurate time and date, a memory card has been inserted, and the battery is fully charged, it becomes suitable for capturing images. However, here are some basic camera operations and settings to start with as a beginner, to enable you capture images and shoot videos right away:

Fully Automatic- Auto Mode

This camera is advantageous if you wish to capture an image without adjusting the settings or if you prefer to delegate most of the control to the camera. Follow these steps if you prefer to have the camera make the majority of the decisions:

1. Detach the lens cover and store the lens in a secure location.

2. Click the On/Off Control. Thereafter, the LCD display will come to life to indicate that the camera has been activated. (When the LCD screen is folded to its closed state, the viewfinder will function instead of the screen itself.)

3. Locate the mode dial atop the camera and rotate it until the white indicator line intersects the green camera icon; this activates the Auto shooting mode.

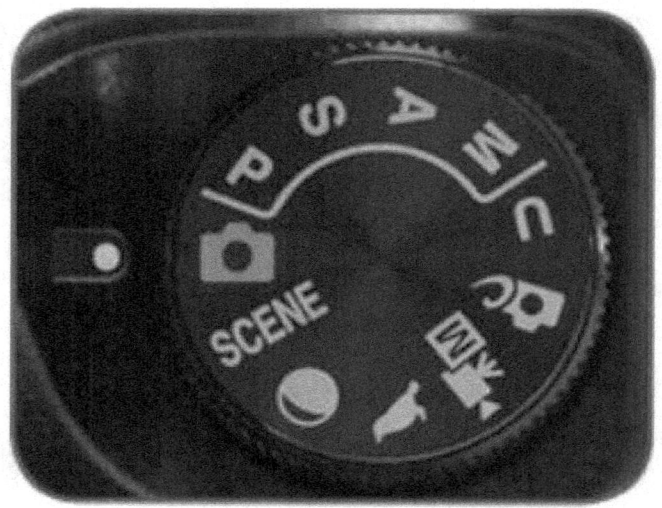

4. Ensure that the focus mode selector, which is a small switch located above the AE/AF Lock button on the upper right side of the camera's rear, is adjusted to the AF position.

5. On the rear of the camera, locate the Menu icon in the lower-left corner of the control area. Navigate to the Shooting Menu (indicated by a camera icon) using the direction controls (four borders of the ridged multi selector dial). Navigate to the Image Quality entry, select that line using the Right-click or OK button, and then press OK while highlighting the Fine setting. After locating the Image Size setting, select it, and opt for the highest resolution option of 4608 x 3456 pixels. To go back to shooting mode, select the Menu button.

Image size

16ᴍ	4608×3456
8ᴍ	3264×2448
4ᴍ	2272×1704
2ᴍ	1600×1200
16:9 12ᴍ	4608×2592
3:2 14ᴍ	4608×3072

6. No action is required to compose an image on the LCD screen located at the rear of the camera, provided that the LCD screen is illuminated and its active surface is exposed. To make the screen visible while the screen is folded against the camera, drag it to the left and rotate it. Press the Monitor button if required to activate it. To switch to the viewfinder, click the Monitor button once more.

7. Utilize the screen or viewfinder to examine the camera's settings and compose the image. To fine-tune the viewfinder to suit your acuity, rotate the diopter adjustment dial located on the left side of the housing of the viewfinder. To transition between the viewfinder and the LCD, utilize the Monitor Button. Note, if the EVF Auto Toggle menu option is enabled, the LCD will be replaced with the viewfinder as the subject's head approaches the viewfinder.

8. To activate the flash when indoors or in other environments where its use might be necessary, locate the lightning bolt-marked control on the left side of the camera, in close proximity to the built-in flash unit.

9. To access the flash mode menu, once the flash has activated, press the Up button on the multi selector, denoted by an additional lightning bolt. Note: Ensure that the Auto settings is selected at the top of this menu.

10. As soon as you have your subject in focus, compose the desired image by examining the LCD screen or the viewfinder window, depending on which option you selected in Step 6

11. Reach out for the Zoom Lever situated on the ring encircling the shutter button in the upper-right corner of the camera's front panel. To obtain a wider-angle picture, move the lever to the left while the indicator points toward the letter W. Alternatively, to obtain a telephoto, zoomed-in shot, move the lever to the right while the indicator points toward the letter T. Alternatively, you can opt to utilize the corresponding zoom lens located on the left side of the lens; by adjusting it upwards, you can achieve telephoto mode and downwards, wide-angle.

12. When the image is appropriately composed, partially press the shutter release button. Note: once you hear a beep and one or more green rectangles is displayed on the screen, it indicates that the image is in focus. Also note that if a red rectangle that flashes indicates that the camera is struggling to achieve

focus; what you should do in this case is to reposition the camera at an alternative angle and subsequently half click the shutter button again.

13. Completely press down the shutter button in order to capture the image.

Note: If you desire greater control over the images you capture, you can set the camera to Program mode. While the camera continues to use its exposure automation as in Auto mode, additional menu options are also accessible by you. Begin by choosing Program Mode with the mode dial, which is located atop the camera.

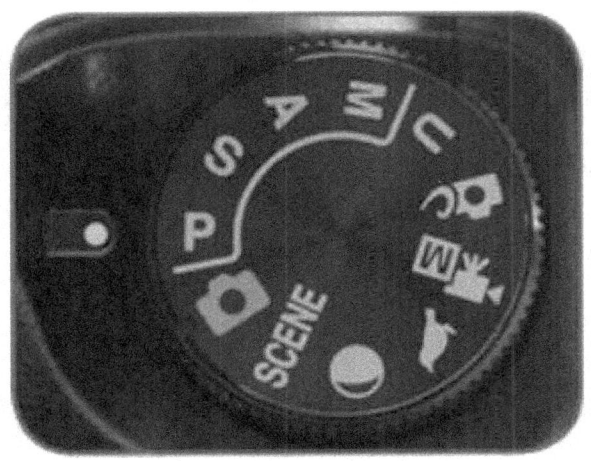

Also note; By selecting the Menu icon, the Shooting menu expands to display an additional set of options. Unlike the Auto mode menu, which consists of two lines, the Shooting menu comprises four displays containing twenty configurable settings. These include white balance, ISO, metering mode, exposure bracketing, and more. The camera determines the appropriate exposure in Program mode, taking into account both the aperture (the size of the opening to allow light) and the shutter speed (the duration for which the shutter remains open to allow light).

Focus

How to choose a standard autofocus mode is detailed below. To commence, tap the Down button denoted by a (flower symbol). This operation displays a compact menu consisting of three options. The letters AF represent typical autofocus, the flower icon represents macro (closeup) focus, and the mountain icon represents focus on infinity.

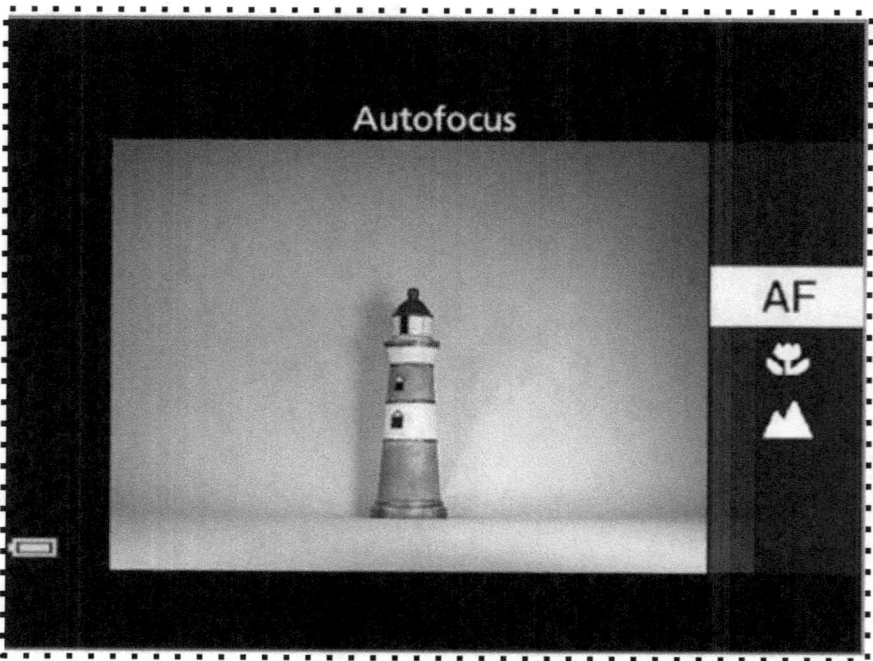

1. In the first stage, select the upper icon via the direction buttons, to enable autofocus. (Note; Time is of the essence; the three options will vanish within a few seconds.) Clicking the OK button will select and verify your selection. Unless the setting is AF, the letters or icon representing your selection will be displayed in the upper left corner of the screen. However, should you choose AF, the letters will only be visible for a brief duration of time before disappearing, as this is the default setting.

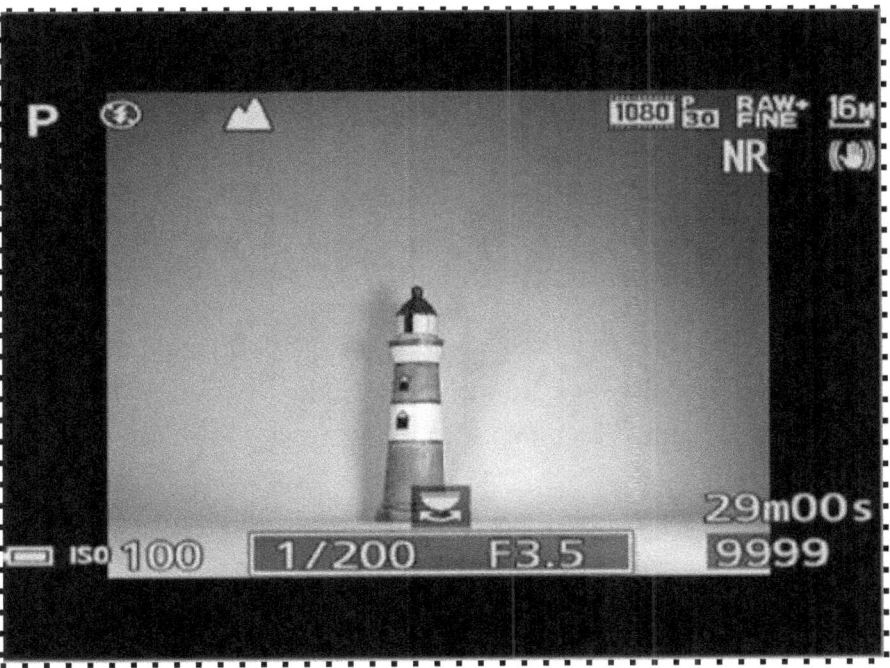

2. To access the shooting options, click on the menu control located at the bottom of the camera's rear. Utilize the Up and Down buttons in conjunction with the selection block to navigate the menu items list until the line corresponding to AF

Area Mode is visually highlighted in yellow on the second screen of the menu.

3. Press OK to select that item, then highlight Manual (Normal) using the Up and Down buttons.

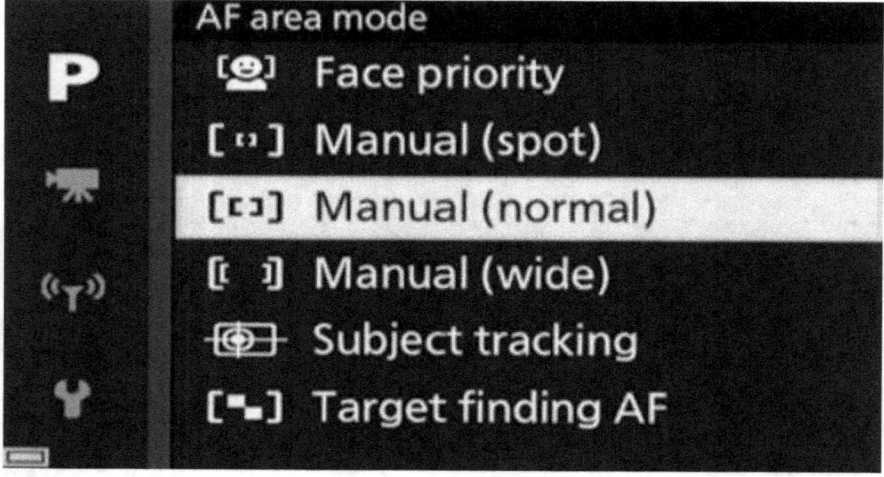

4. To proceed to the shooting display, hold the shutter button halfway after confirming the selection with the OK button. There should be a focus frame containing four arrows at this point.

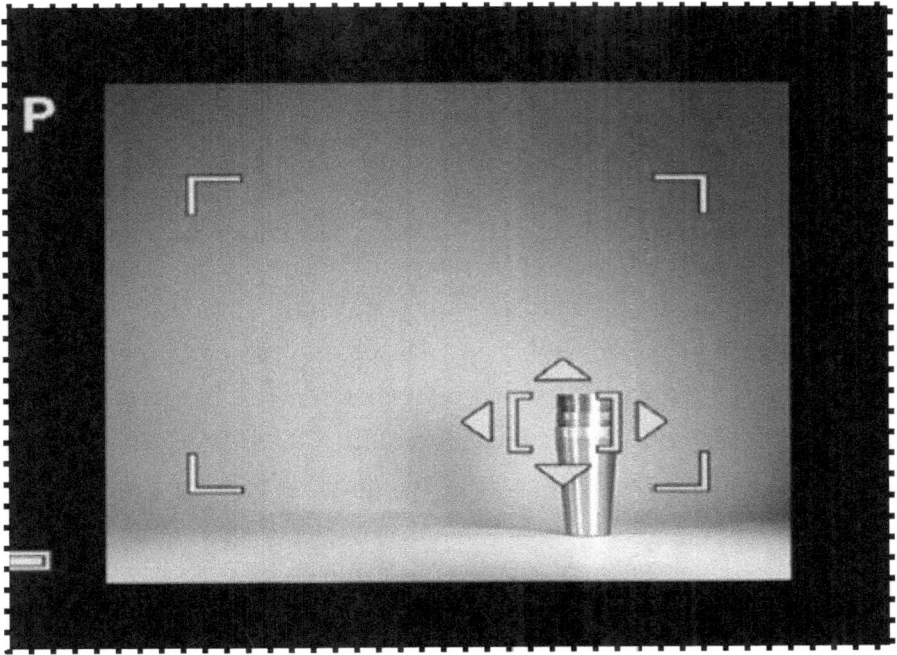

5. However, should in case you don't see the arrows at this point, click the OK button to make them visible.

6. The camera will center a focus frame in the center of the screen when this option is selected. Using the multi selector dial or the direction controls, you can move the frame around the screen; pressing OK to affirm will secure the focus frame in the position it was before you clicked on OK.

7. Aim the camera with the subject centered between the white focus brackets.

8. Partially press the shutter button to enable the camera to assess the exposure and focus. To verify the focus, a chime should sound and the focus brackets should change color to green.

9. Once you are sure that everything settings is accurate, fully depress the shutter button in order to capture the image.

Note this situation: Assuming you decide to capture an image in which the subject does not occupy the screen's center. Or perhaps the image is composed of a person positioned to the right of center, with an attractive scenery extending to the left of the frame. Position the focus frame over the subject to be captured, which is the individual positioned to the right in this instance. Partially press down the shutter button until the camera comes into focus and emits a sound. Maintaining the button halfway depressed will secure the focus and exposure as you maneuver the camera to the left, positioning the subject at the right, in order to achieve the intended composition. Afterwards, when you capture the photograph, the area that was initially in focus will remain so.

Manual Focus

Manual focus is an alternative major focusing method. Numerous photographers appreciate the degree of control that enables them to precisely adjust the focus. In certain circumstances, such as focusing in low-light conditions or behind obstructions like wire fences or glass, capturing extreme close-ups, or situations involving objects positioned at different distances from the camera, the ability to precisely regulate the location of the point of sharpest focus could be important.

To utilize manual focus, position the focus mode selector to the MF setting (located above the AE/AF Lock button). Upon initial selection of the manual focus mode, the screen is initially presented at its standard magnification, and thereafter it would be increased to magnification which is two or four times the standard magnification.

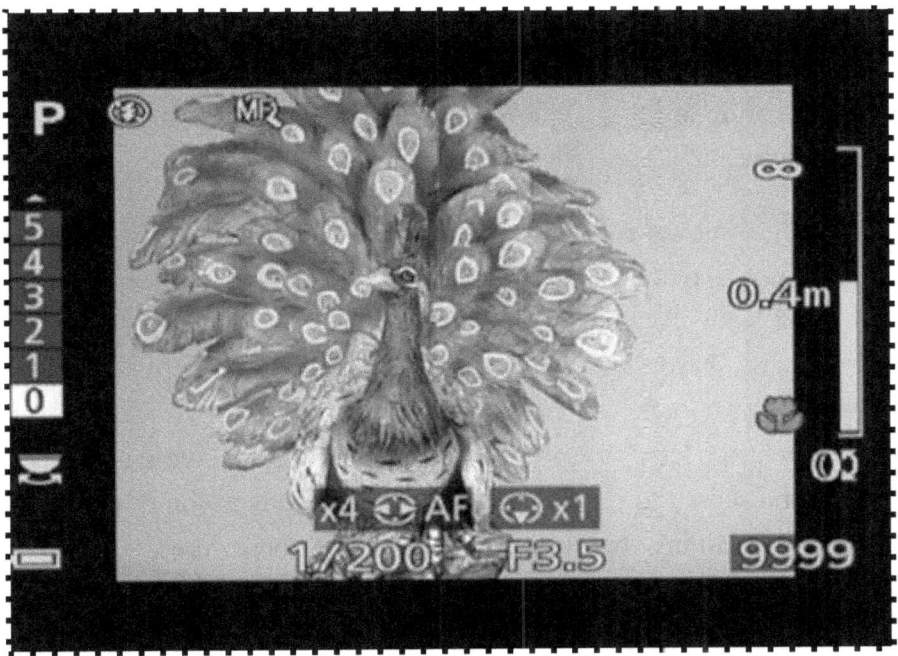

For manual focus, the shooting screen will be displayed when the focus mode selector is initially moved to the MF position. The icons that appear immediately above the aperture and shutter speed values at the bottom of the screen represent the controls that can be utilized to adjust the screen's magnification. This is how it can be decoded:

When the number 4 appears in the leftmost position, 2x magnification is active; to change to 4x magnification, select the Left button. A

43

display of the number 2 indicates that 1x magnification is active; to change to 2x magnification, select the Left button. The number 1 indicates that the magnification is set to 4x; to change to 1x magnification, select the Left button.

When manual focus is selected, the magnification level is retained from the previous manual focus operation. Consequently, when the focus mode selector is positioned in the MF position, the magnification level will change in accordance with the most recently utilized setting.

Start adjusting the focus by rotating the multi selector dial once the camera enters manual focus mode. Turn the dial corresponding to the focusing scale located on the right side of the screen in order to achieve the sharpest possible focus. The instructions provided in the lower left corner of the screen indicate how to adjust the magnification level by pressing the Left button. Alternatively, to return the screen to its normal scale (indicated as x1 on the display) while maintaining the current setting as the focus, press the Down button. You can revert the screen to its original magnification by pressing the Down button. To proceed with altering the focus on the magnified screen, click the Down button once more.

As the focus point is adjusted via the multi selector dial, a white bar within the focus scale will ascend and descend. When the focus is in the macro, or close-up, range, the bar turns green. Continue to make adjustments until you obtain the necessary optimal sharpness and focus for your image, thereafter proceed to capture your photo.

To revert the screen to its standard size and secure focus before using the multi-selector dial for another purpose, such as adjusting aperture in Aperture Priority mode, press the Down button. To return to manual focus adjustment, press the Down button once more.

To utilize the camera's autofocus settings, select the Right button when prompted on the screen. Doing so will cause the camera to focus automatically on the subject located in the center of the screen. Then, manual focus adjustments can be continued by utilizing the multi selector dial.

The control ring, which is a sizable ridged ring encircling the lens, can also be utilized to modify the focus. Simply rotate the ring to achieve precise focus. Manual focus is also possible with the side zoom control if that function has been assigned to the control via the Assign Side Zoom Control option on the second screen of the Setup menu.

Note: When you activate the Peaking function in the last display of the Setup menu, the command dial can be utilized to modify the magnitude of the Peaking effect as indicated by the numerical scale to the left of the screen. This function shows a progressive enlargement of white pixels in the regions of sharp focus as the level of focus increases.

Exposure (Exposure Compensation)

The Program mode and Auto mode of the Coolpix P950 are both effective at selecting optimal exposure for your image. However, there are circumstances in which overriding the camera's automatic exposure settings is necessary.

Exposure compensation is a practical means that can be employed to address atypical or suboptimal lighting conditions. For example, if your subject is positioned in front of a white background, the auto exposure function of the camera will produce an overly dark exposure to compensate for the expansive white area. One way to address this issue involves utilizing the exposure compensation control of the camera. Note: Try to observe the label adjacent to the Right button on the multi-selector dial. This label bears small plus and negative signs, the former set against a black background and the latter set against a white one. By pressing this button, the exposure compensation option is engaged, allowing the user to manually adjust the exposure to a certain extent.

Choose the Program mode and Focus on your subject. When you press the Right button, a vertical scale with +2.0 at the top and -2.0 at the bottom will appear on the right side of the display.

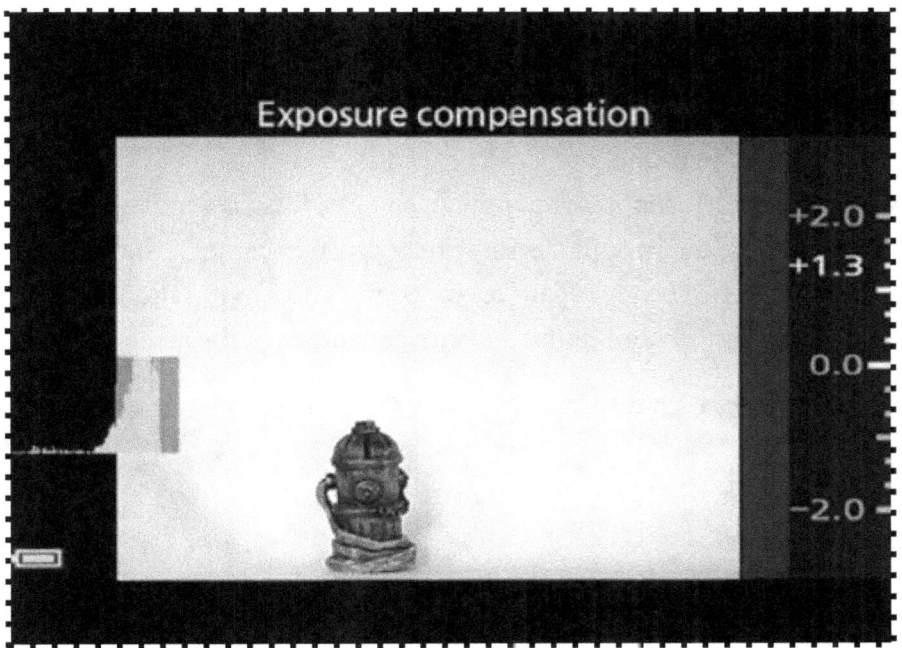

To adjust the value displayed on the exposure compensation scale, press the Up and Down buttons, rotate the multi selector dial, or use the command dial. The value being adjusted is denoted by yellow check marks that appear on the scale. By repositioning the yellow markers to the very bottom of the scale, the resulting image will be significantly darkened in contrast to the outcome produced by the automatic exposure feature. Placing the yellow check marks at the top of the image will result in a discernible increase in brightness.

The screen of the camera alternates between brightness and darkness to indicate the changing exposure which occurs before you capture an image. On the left side of the screen, the camera also displays a histogram graph, which visually represents the lighting values as peaks and valleys.

Note: In order to avoid inadvertently affecting subsequent photographs, you should reset the exposure compensation to zero in the center of the scale after capturing your first image. Caution should be exercised in this regard, as the exposure compensation value set on the camera will continue to apply even after it is powered off and on again. The camera will display the exposure compensation value, whether positive or negative, in conjunction with the exposure compensation symbol, in the lower right corner of the screen.

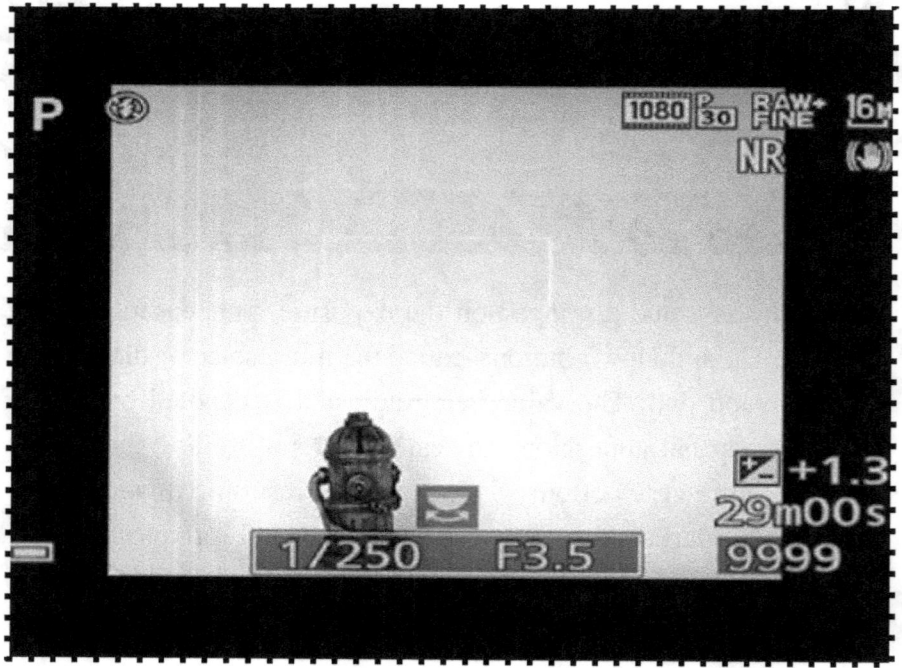

Motion Picture Recording

To utilize the Motion Picture Recording Options, follow the steps below

1. While the camera is in Auto mode, ensure the flash unit button
    is turned off, as the flash will not be utilized. Immediately you
    turn on your camera, position the yellow selection block in the
    line of icons at the far left of the screen, by pressing the Menu
    button followed by the Left button. Browse through to reach
    the second icon, which resembles a movie camera, select it
    and press the Right button to return the selection rectangle to
    the menu. This Movie interface screen contains six items
    which are available for capturing video footage.

2. Browse through to reach the last option on the menu screen
    labeled "Frame Rate" and select it by pressing the Right button
    or OK button. This will bring you to a screen containing two
    options for this configuration: 25 fps (25p/50p) or 30 fps
    (30p/60p).

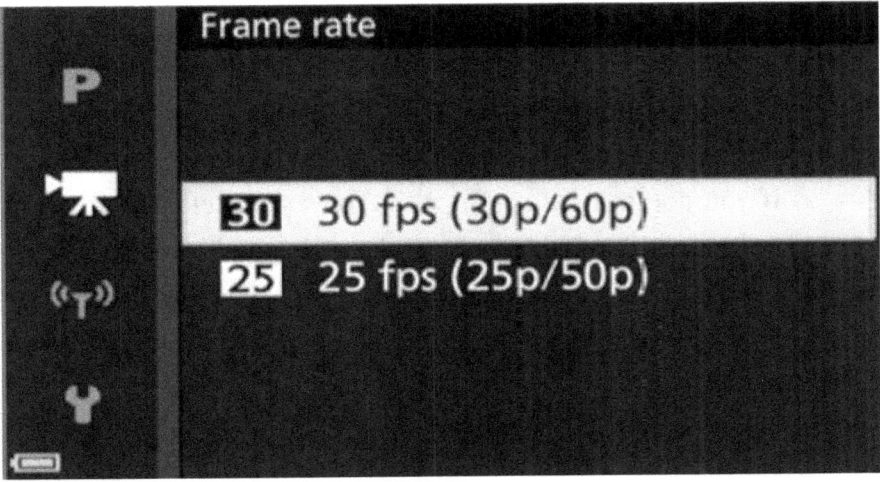

3. The frames per second upon which the camera will shoot
    video in the highest-quality (HD) formats are determined by

this setting. The benchmark for the NTSC video system, which is utilized in the United States, Canada, Mexico, Japan, and other countries, is 30 frames per second. The 25 fps preset is the PAL video system standard, which is utilized throughout Europe and other regions. Unless there are compelling reasons to change, select the 30 fps option if you are located in the United States. This configuration will influence the available choices for the Movie Options item.

4. Proceed to the Movie Options at the top of the menu screen, select it by pressing the OK button or the Right button to proceed to the subsequent screen, and examine the list of available choices. The number 30 or 60 will appear among the initial five options on this screen if you set the Frame Rate to 30 fps. But the number 25 or 50 will appear in the first five options, if you have chosen 25 frames per second.

5. Select the second option for Movie Options, which is 1080/30p if you selected 30 fps for the frame rate. The Frame Rate menu will be set to 25fps, if the second item is 1080/25p. If you do not have a compelling reason to select that option, revert to 30 frames per second. By utilizing this mode, one can effortlessly capture movies in 4K without the complexities associated with employing the most advanced setting, which is indicated as 2160/30p in the menu.

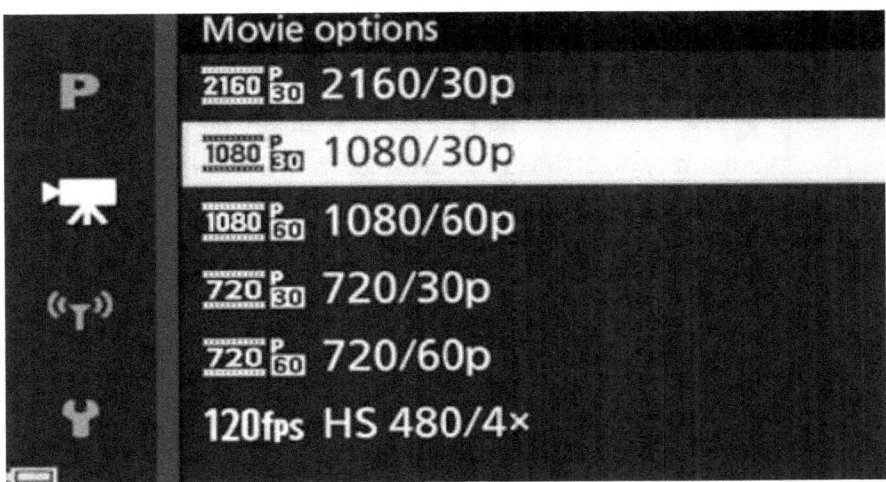

6. Proceed to the Autofocus Mode option, which is the second choice on the Movie menu screen. To proceed to the subsequent screen, press the Right button or the OK button and choose the Full time AF option in the second list.

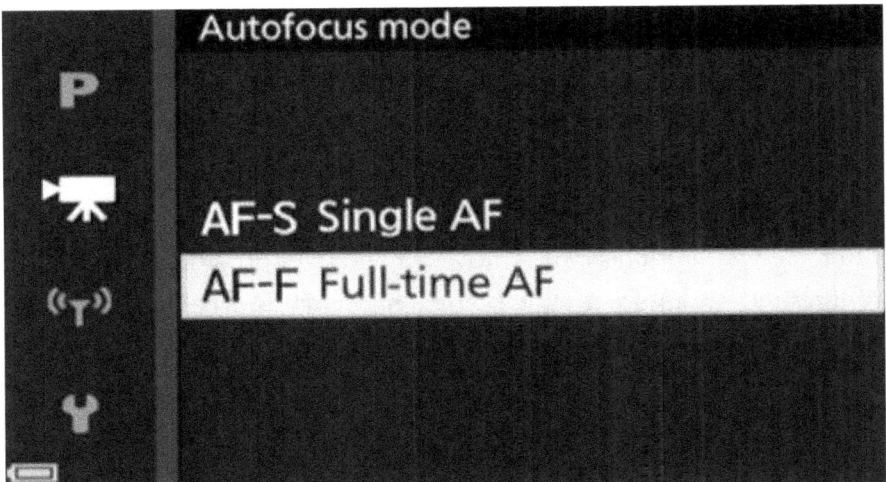

7. Confirm this selection by pressing the OK button. By selecting this option, the camera will dynamically adjust its focus in response to changes in the distance between itself and the main subject. Then, if desired, return to the Movie menu and enable the Zoom Microphone and Electronic VR. To go away from the menu options, tap the menu button.

8. Once the image is in the desired composition, select the red Movie button once more. (This button is located below the AE/AF Lock button, near the top of the camera's rear.) It is unnecessary to continue to hold down the shutter; simply press and leave it. The camera's display will momentarily go black, after which the remaining minutes and seconds for the recording will be displayed in the lower right alongside a red REC indicator in the upper left.

Note: Till the Camera gets to a recording limit or until you press the red button again to halt the recording, the camera will continue to shoot. Also note that the camera will alter the exposure automatically in response to changing lighting conditions. Additionally, unless there is a compelling reason not to, maintain maximum camera stability (if feasible, utilize a tripod or monopod). Restrict camera movement to fluid, slow motions, such as a pan (side-to-side motion) to progressively capture a wide scene, and avoid unnecessary zooming or panning.

VIEWING PICTURES AND MOVIES

Review While in Shooting Mode

If you have the Monitor Settings option of the Setup menu set to enable the Image Review function, each time you capture a still image, the captured image will briefly appear on the screen (or in the viewfinder if it is in use). After a new photograph is taken, the image will remain on the screen for approximately one second by default.

Reviewing Images In Playback Mode

In order to access previously captured images, activate playback mode by selecting the Playback button located to the right of the LCD screen. This button is denoted by a small triangle icon. By rotating the multi selector dial or the Left and Right or Up and Down controls on the selector, one can navigate through the captured images. Using the direction controls and the zoom mechanism located on top of the camera, you can magnify and navigate through any image that has been magnified. To navigate through the images at a faster rate, press and hold any of the four direction controls.

Also observe that, some images that were captured via the camera's continuous photography functions will bear the labeling of "OK" followed by a colon and a triangle in the bottom center. Pressing the OK button will "open" a series of continuous photos; to navigate between the pictures in that series, use the direction buttons. Press the

Up icon to return to the primary viewing screen, where you can view additional images and sequences of images.

Playing Movies

If you want to replay motion pictures, navigate through the previously captured images using the aforementioned methods until you locate an image that has an icon in the lower right corner of the screen and also has a video format, such as 1080p, and a file name which ends in mp4.

Press the OK button while the frame from the movie is being shown on the screen, to initiate playback of the film on the LCD or, if the electronic viewfinder is active in place of the LCD, in the electronic viewfinder. You will also see a row of DVR-like controls, located in the lower left corner of the display.

Utilize the direction buttons to navigate the series of options. To activate one of the options, select one by using the direction button and press OK. Additionally, the multi selector dial can be rotated to the left to rewind or to the right to fast forward. To adjust the intensity of the audio, rotate the zoom lever (located around the stop button) in the direction of the T position (indicating increased loudness) or the W position (indicating decreased softness). When you modify the sound, a small set of volume "waves", either an increase or decrease will appear beside the speaker icon in the lower right corner of the display. It should be noted, however, that if the camera is connected to a television, this control will not allow you to modify the sound level. In such a case, you will need to utilize the volume control on the television.

You can playback or edit videos on your computer via applications like iMovie for the Macintosh or any other Mac or Windows program capable of processing video files ending in.mp4. Sometimes, certain video editing software for Windows requires the P950's movie files to be converted to the.avi format prior to importation. One possible application for accomplishing this is mp4cam2avi, which is accessible via the web at http://mp4cam2avi.sourceforge.net/. Additionally, the ViewNX Movie Editor software, which is included with the ViewNX-i product from Nikon, can be utilized.

Autofocus Modes

Focal plane contrast AF is an autofocus feature used by the camera, which detects contrast at the pixel level using information directly obtained from the imaging sensor. This is referred to simply as contrast-detect AF. Autofocus can be achieved by utilizing the entire surface area of the imaging sensor to distinguish between light and dark boundaries. As it operates at the pixel level, this form of autofocus is comparatively sluggish, but it is incredibly precise.

Although, an earlier introductory section of this book has provided a synopsis of the Autofocus feature, which is a fundamental operation of the camera. However, in this section, emphasis would be placed on providing detailed explanations of each mode in the camera Auto Focus feature. Always keep in mind that the Autofocus modes instruct the camera on how to focus. Follow the instructions below to select an Autofocus mode:

1. Utilize the i icon to access the Information display screen, then choose Autofocus mode from the Quick Menu located on the right.

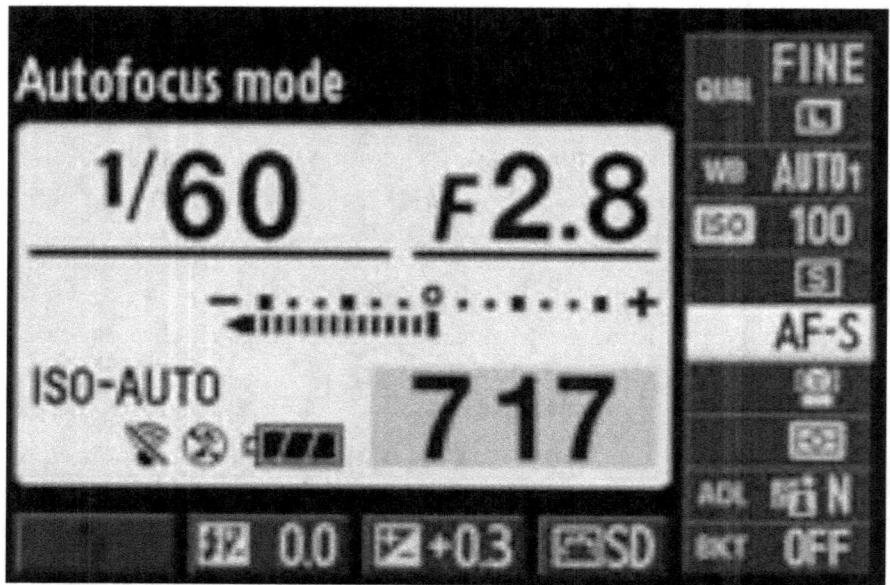

2. When you press the OK button, the Autofocus mode menu will appear. Choose the Autofocus mode setting that you prefer. Once more, press the OK button to confirm your selection.

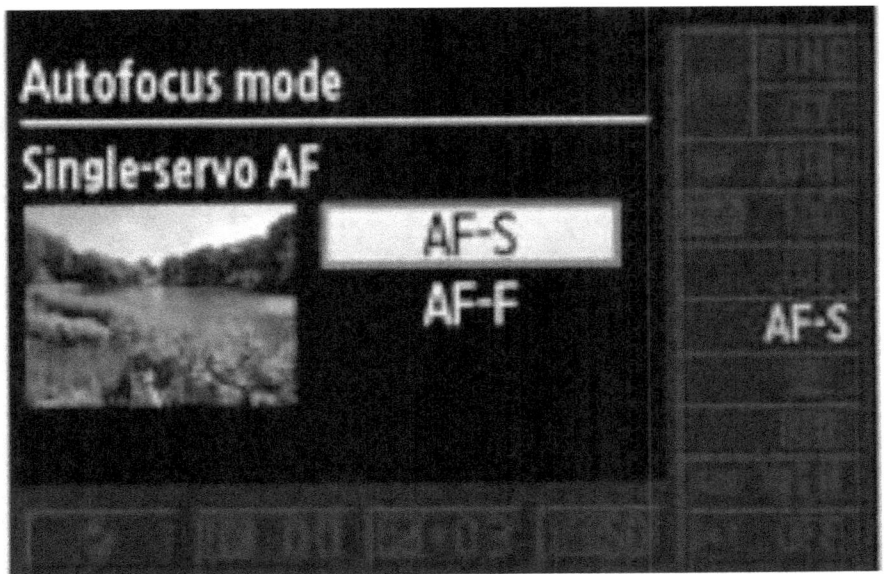

3. Initiate the Live view interface by partially pressing and releasing the shutter button. Upon doing so, the Autofocus mode selection that you previously made will be reflected on the Live view interface. After that, commence the process of capturing your photographs.

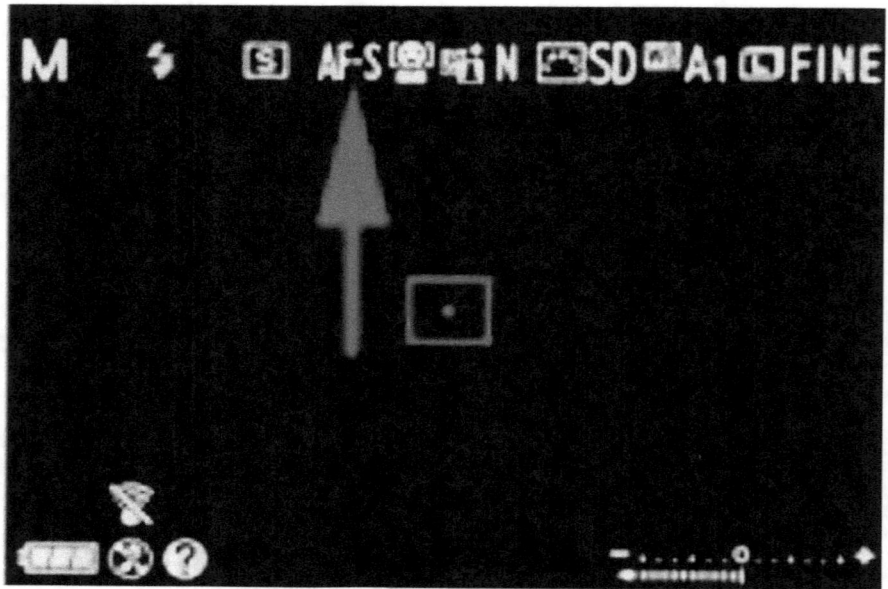

Single-Servo (AF-S)

By partially depressing the Shutter-release button while in still image or video mode, the focus can be adjusted.

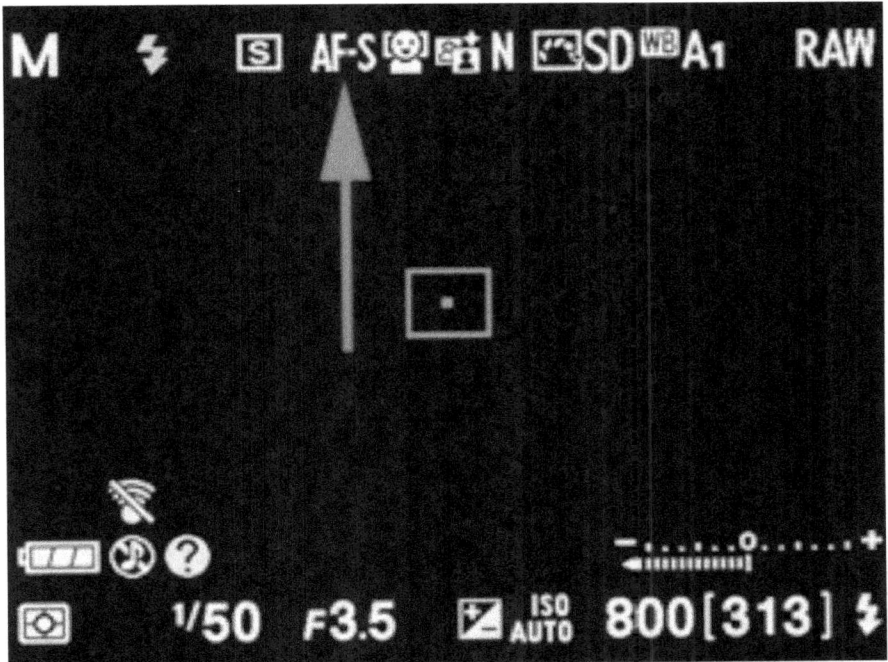

To refocus the camera when the subject moves, you must release the shutter button and partially press it again to put the camera in focus again. The focus becomes fixed and remains so, unless an intentional update is performed. Note; Refocusing the camera is required whenever the subject or the photographer changes position.

Note; A large AF point square, either green or red, will appear in the center of the camera's display. A dot will be present in the square when it is positioned in the center of the display. It will be colored green when the scene is in focus and red when it is not. By dragging the square across the display, one can designate the region of the subject that will be brought into focus by the camera. Use this AF mode if the subject remains stationary or moves very slowly; it permits you to refocus at will.

Full-Time Servo AF (AF-F)

As in Single-servo AF mode, the red or green AF point square appears in the center of the camera's display.

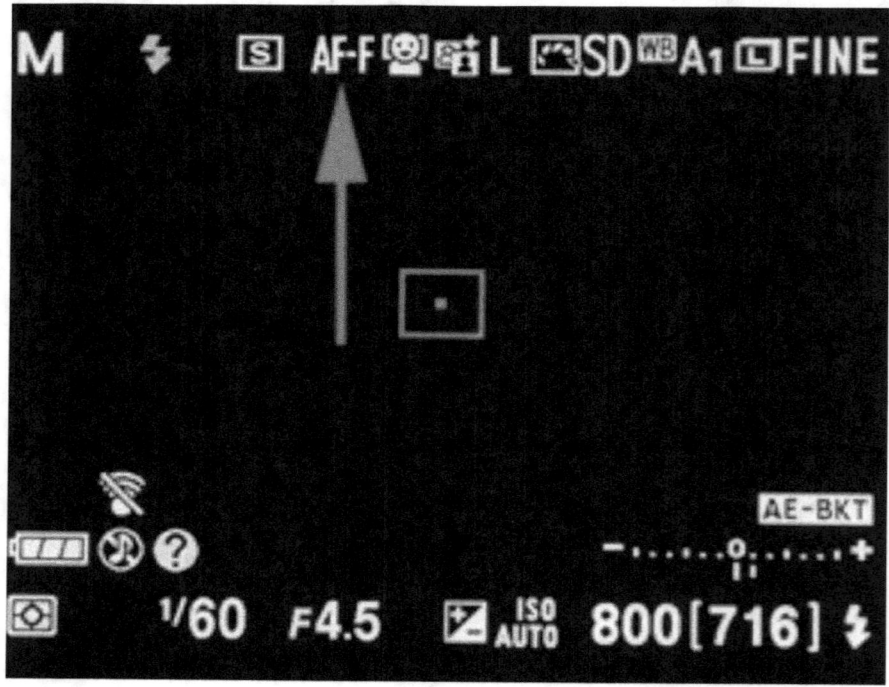

It is capable of being moved to determine the focus area. This mode updates the autofocus continuously in order to monitor the subject. It is influenced by the specified AF-area mode. The subject is not the focal point; instead, it undergoes continuous updates unless the Shutter-release button is partially depressed to initiate a refocus. In other words, the camera will autonomously sustain focus on the subject while in AF-F mode. However, if the image loses focus, it is possible to regain it by partially tapping the shutter-release button.

Not; It is recommended to completely press the shutter-release button in still image mode to commence the shooting of your pictures. Also, fully press the Shutter-release button in Movie mode to initiate and terminate a video recording.

Aside from extremely specialized macro photography, the Autofocus mode should remain set to AF-S, or Single-servo AF. AF-F mode can be advantageous when shooting videos with autofocus (rather than manual focus); nevertheless, it has a tendency to lose focus at times; therefore, you will need to test its effectiveness with your subjects.

Utilizing autofocus on a camera is an absolute delight. It demonstrates efficiency even in low light, albeit with a slightly increased effort, and is quite quick when illuminated adequately.

Although the system may still appear complicated at times, dedicating some time to this section should provide you with a significantly enhanced comprehension of the AF modes. You will also gain an understanding of how to modify your camera to complement your photographic approach.

AF-AREA MODES

In the AF-area mode, the location where the camera detects the subject can be modified. The operation of autofocus varies among the four AF-area configurations. One has the ability to direct the camera to detect faces, monitor moving subjects, adjust the aperture for landscapes, or concentrate on a specific region of the frame. After demonstrating how to select an AF-area mode, we will examine them in depth. Follow the instructions below to modify the AF-area mode:

1. Using the i icon to access the Information display screen, navigate to the Quick Menu on the right and select AF-area mode.

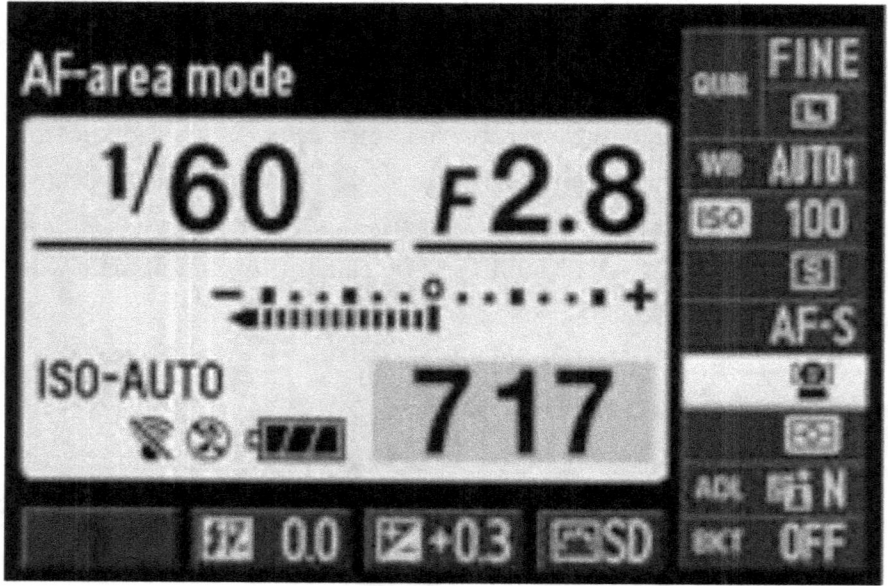

2. When you press the OK button, the AF-area mode menu will appear. Choose your preferred AF-area mode configuration. Once more, press the OK button to confirm your selection.

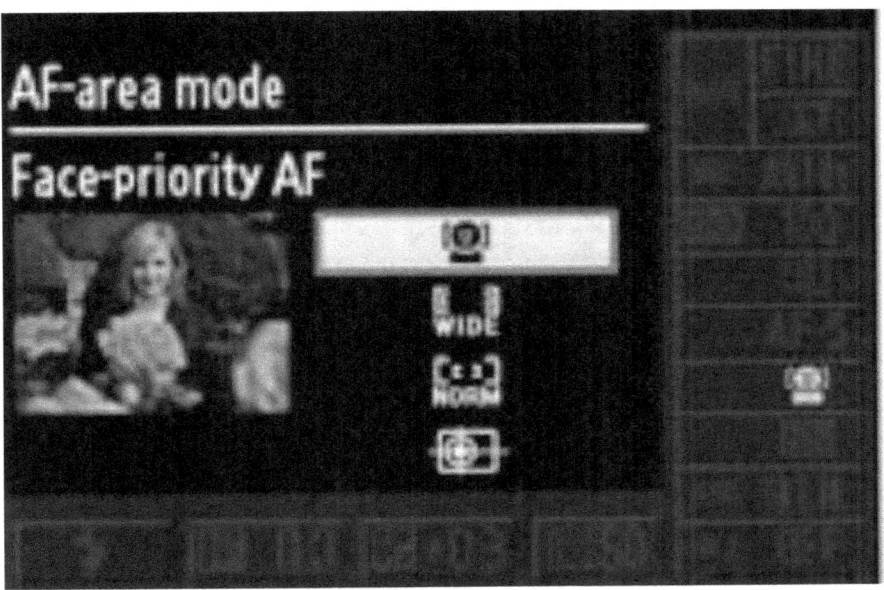

3. Return to the Live view display by partially pressing the Shutter-release button; the AF-area mode selection you made will be displayed on the Live view display. You may then proceed with shooting your photographs or recordings.

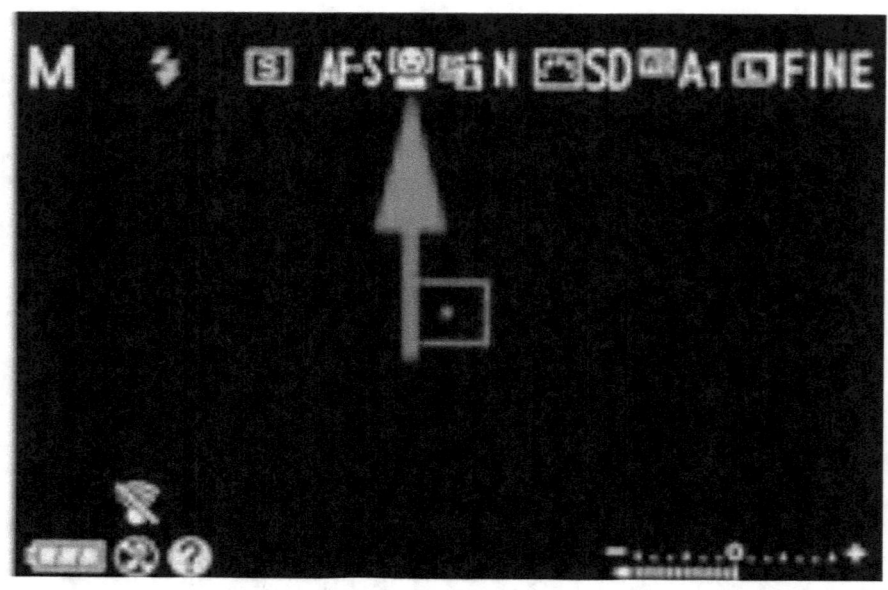

Face-Priority AF

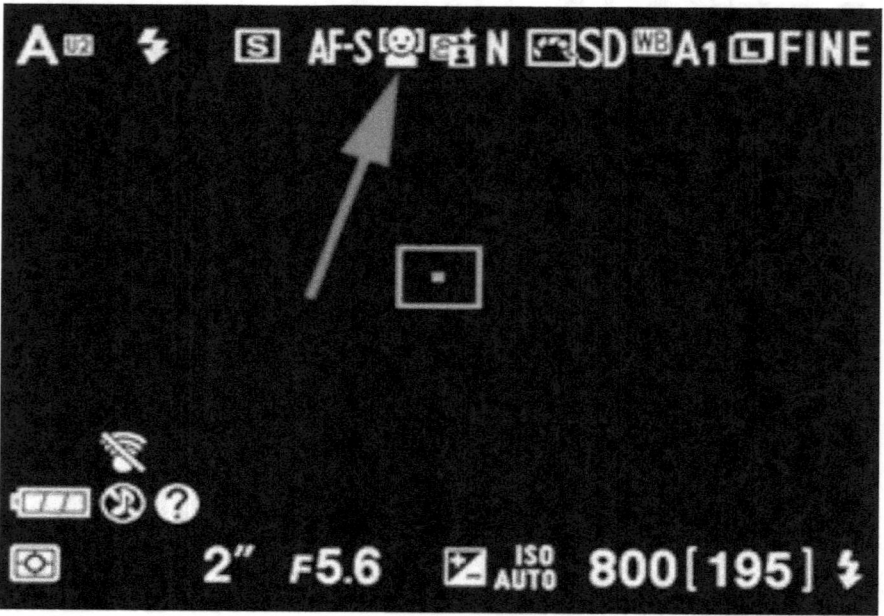

Face-priority AF should be utilized when taking portraits in Live view mode or filming with individuals in Movie mode. The camera is capable of tracking focus on the faces of multiple individuals simultaneously. Note; you need to observe as the green and yellow AF point squares locate and monitor moving faces; green squares indicate features that are in sharp focus, while yellow squares indicate individuals who are being tracked but are not in the best of focus.

Nikon claims the camera is capable of simultaneously detecting up to 35 images. Thus as was written in their website; "When multiple faces are detected, the camera will focus on the subject identified as the closest".

However, the Multi Selector can be utilized to select an alternative subject which you want to be the main focus.

Wide-Area AF

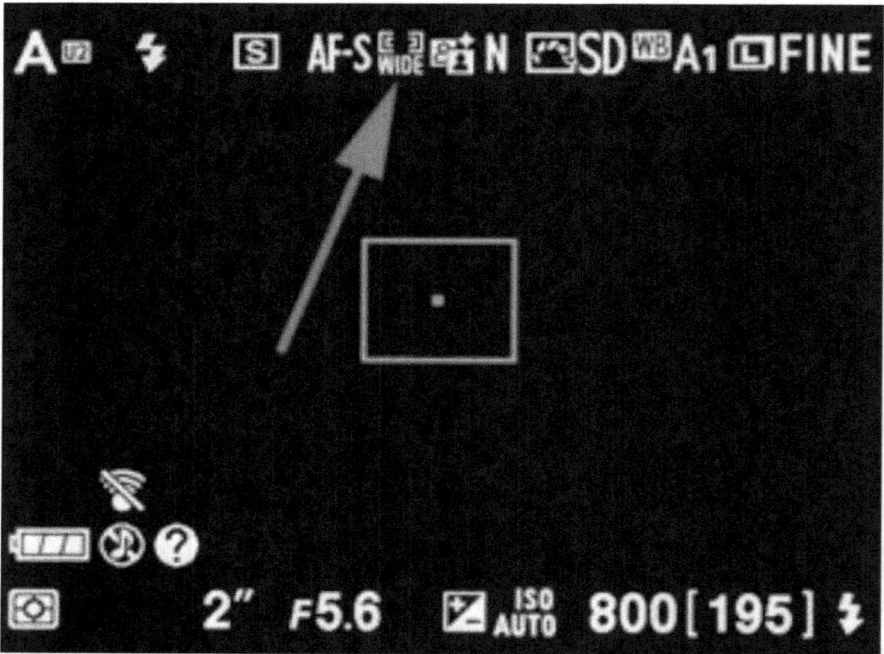

This mode is for the landscape photographers among us who enjoy capturing still images or videos of breathtaking scenery. On the monitor, the camera will exhibit a sizable AF point rectangle. It is possible to adjust the position of this sizable AF point until it precisely locks onto the desired focus point. The camera will determine the optimal focus by sensing a broad area, giving priority to the region beneath the AF rectangle.

This AF-area mode, according to Nikon, is "appropriate for handheld photography, including landscape shots". Note: It is possible to adjust the AF area to any position within the frame.

Normal- Area AF

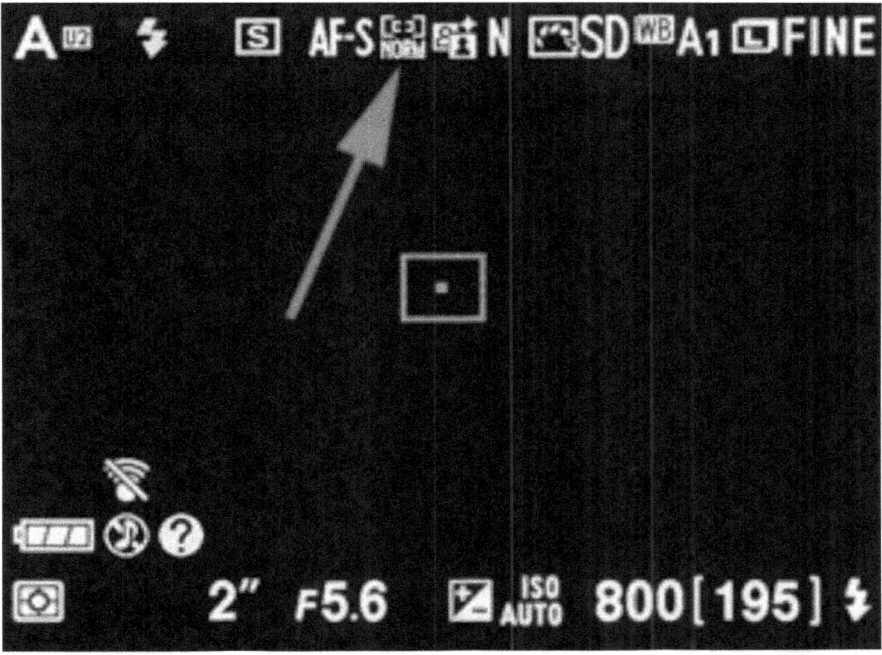

This mode is designed for photographers who require extremely precise focus on a small portion of the frame. For instance, if you wish to focus on one of the antennae while photographing a close-up of a butterfly, utilize Normal-area AF. This mode is ideal for macro (closeup) photos because the AF point square is considerably smaller and can be moved around the frame.

When contrasting the square with the AF point in Wide-area AF mode, one will observe that the square is approximately 25 percent smaller in size. It is possible to precisely define the region of the subject that requires the most pronounced focus.

This AF-area mode, according to Nikon, is "appropriate for tripod photography involving pin-point focus, such as close-ups". Note; It is possible to adjust the AF area to any position within the frame.

Subject-Tracking AF

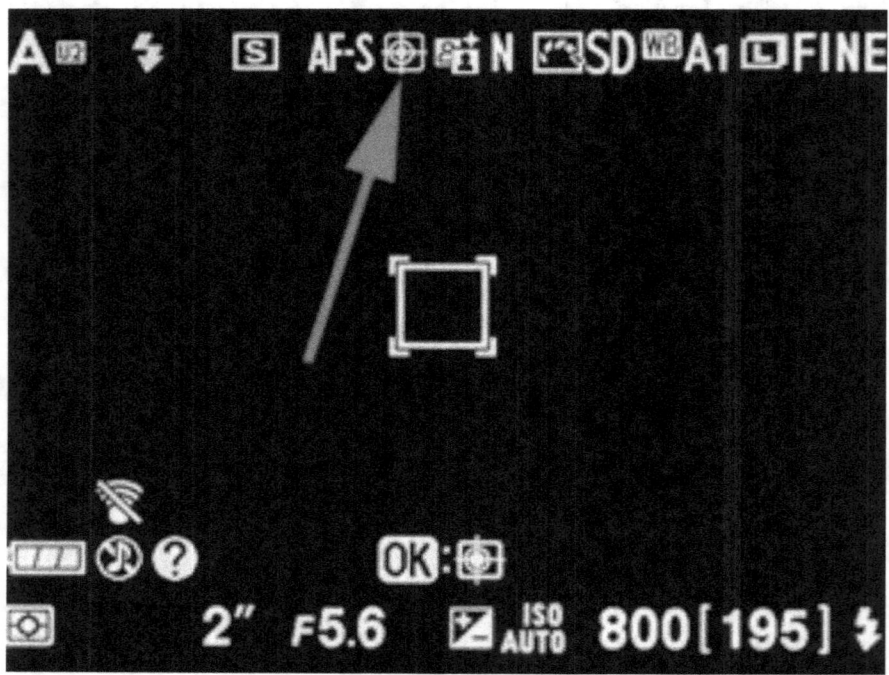

When the autofocus is engaged, either manually in AF-F mode or automatically in AF-S mode, this mode enables the user to initiate subject tracking by pressing the OK button. Upon subject selection (following the press of the OK button), the camera maintains focus on the subject and initiates tracking, irrespective of any motion exhibited by the subject or the camera.

Note: For example, if you want to maintain focus on a black bear in the Great Smoky Mountains while filming a scene featuring the bear, adjust the focus point to the bear, select the OK button, and the image will remain in focus. It is recommended that AF-F, or Full-time servo AF, be utilized in conjunction with this mode. With full-time autofocus, the camera follows the subject automatically, relieving you of the responsibility of manually focusing it.

Additionally, Nikon states that this AF-area mode is "appropriate for subjects in motion". Once focusing is accomplished by pressing the OK button, the subject's movement is tracked by the AF area.

Note; If you frequently photograph individuals, leave the AF-area mode set to Face-priority AF. Also, when employing Live view for macro photography, the Normal-area AF setting provides the most precise and limited area for precise and up-close focusing. Wildlife and sports photographers should utilize Subject-tracking AF, while landscape photographers should employ Wide-area AF.

RELEASE MODES

By utilizing release modes, one can instruct the camera on how to release the shutter when capturing images or filming videos. The following are the six release modes:

1. Single frame (S)

2. Continuous

3. Self-timer

4. Delayed remote (ML-L3)

5. Quick-response (ML-L3)

6. Movie recording

The procedures required to select a Release mode are as follows:

1. Utilize the i icon to access the Information display screen, then choose Release mode from the Quick Menu located to the right.

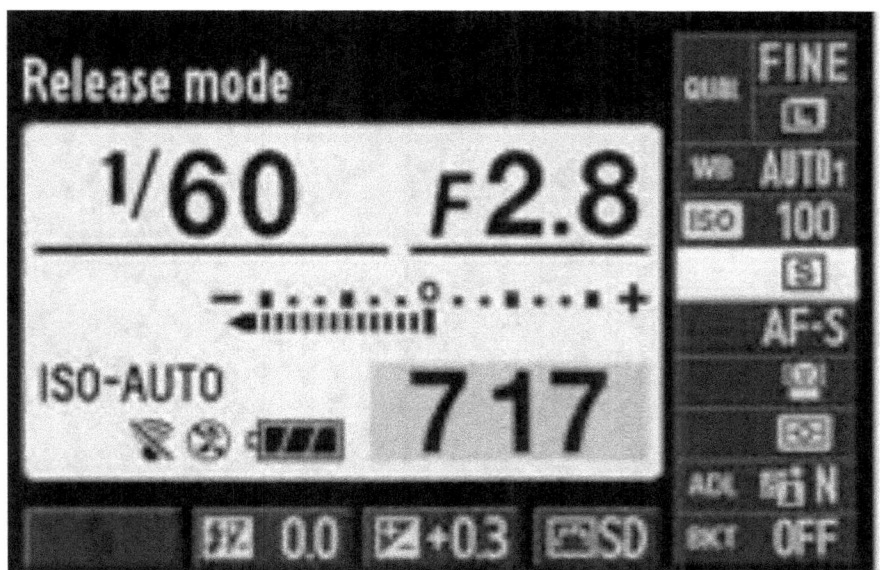

2. When you press the OK button, the Release mode menu will appear. Choose your preferred Release mode configuration. Once more, press the OK button to confirm your selection.

71

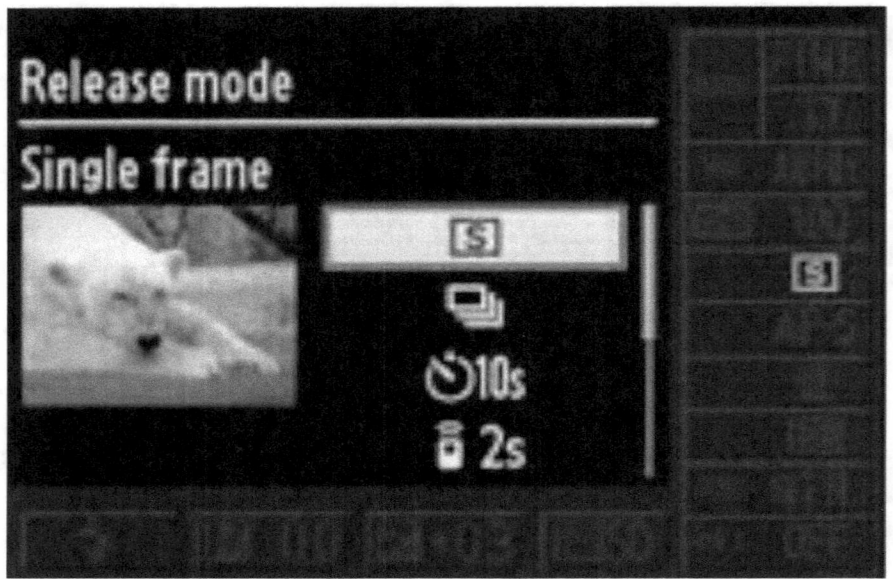

3. On the Live view screen, the Release mode selection you made will be visible after you press the Shutter-release button midway to return to the Live view interface. Thereafter, proceed with your photography or filming.

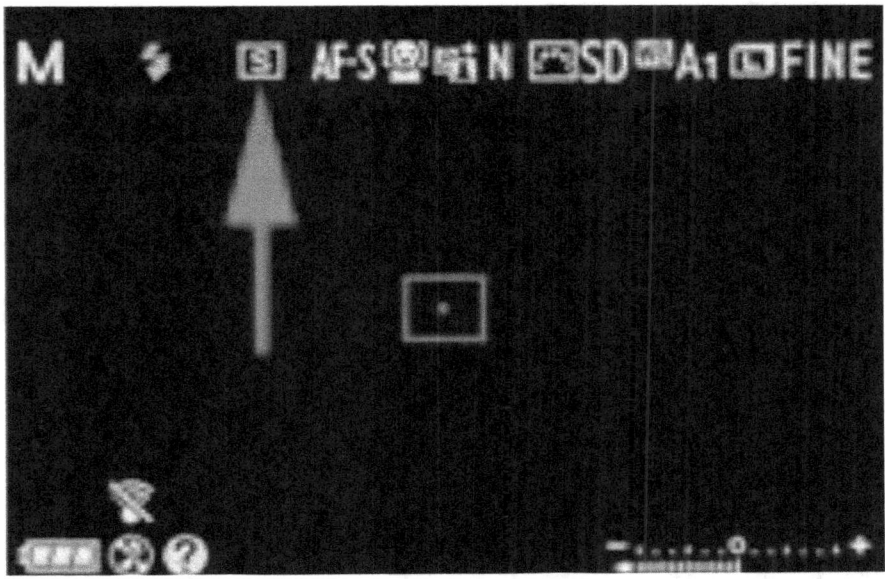

Let us now analyze the Live view mode and the functions of every Release mode.

Single Frame (S) Release Mode

The most basic release mode is the Single Release Mode. Under this mode, a solitary image is captured with each complete stroke of the shutter-release trigger. This is intended for photographers who capture only a few photographs. This mode is frequently employed by nature photographers who prioritize proper depth of field and composition.

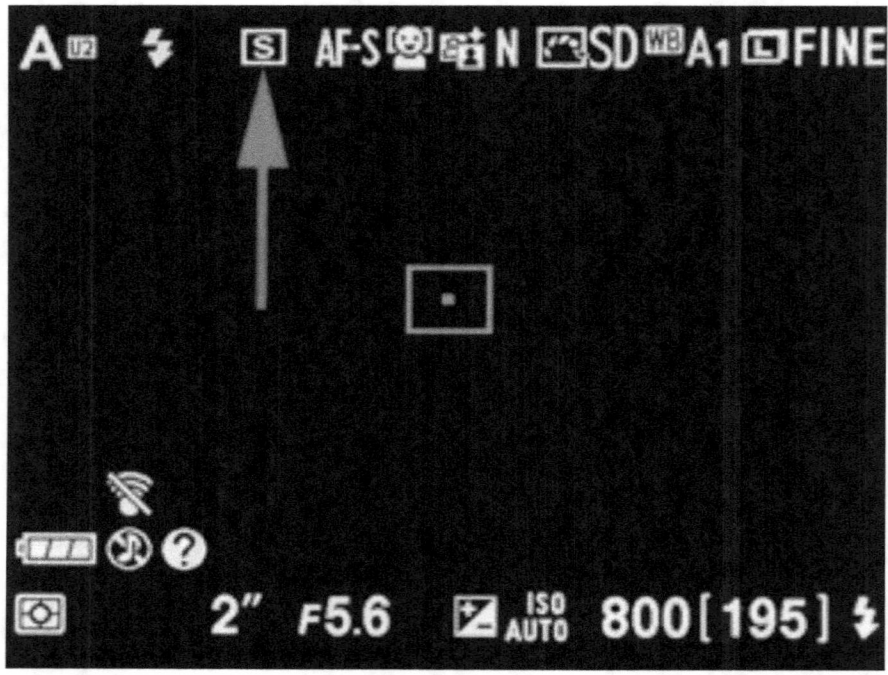

Continuous Release Mode

Continuous Release mode permits burst shooting at a maximum of four frames per second (fps).

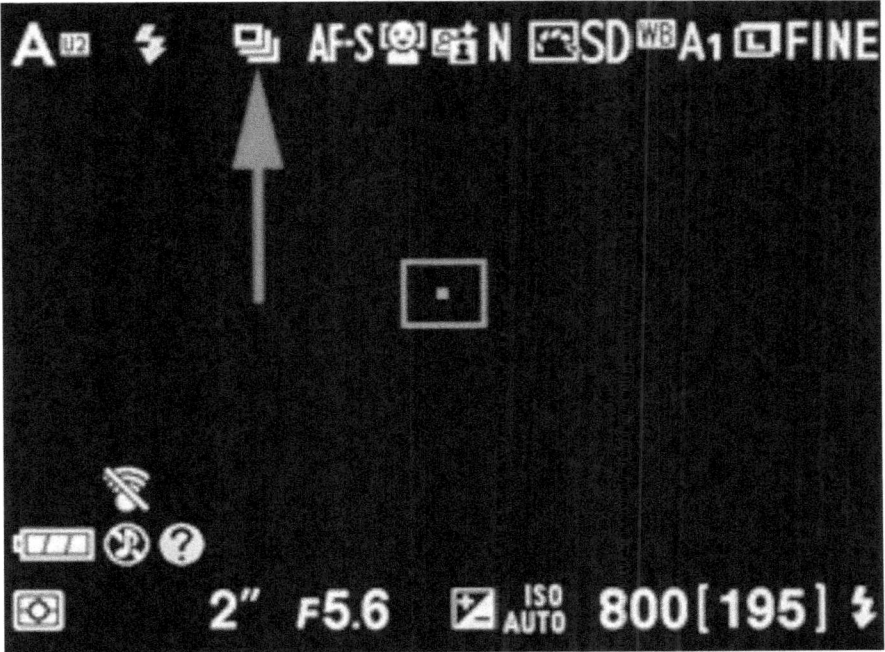

In order to achieve a high frame rate (high fps), the following conditions must be met: a completely charged camera battery, a minimum 1/250 second shutter speed, and available buffer capacity in the memory of the camera.

If these conditions are fulfilled, it is possible to capture multiple images in rapid succession at a rate of up to 4 frames per second. The camera will utilize internal memory to buffer the images prior to committing them to the memory card. As a result of compression proportions, the number of images that can be stored in the internal memory buffer differs depending on whether the subject is basic or complex and whether RAW or JPEG mode is being used. The camera will indicate the remaining number of frames that can be captured prior to the internal memory buffer reaching capacity.

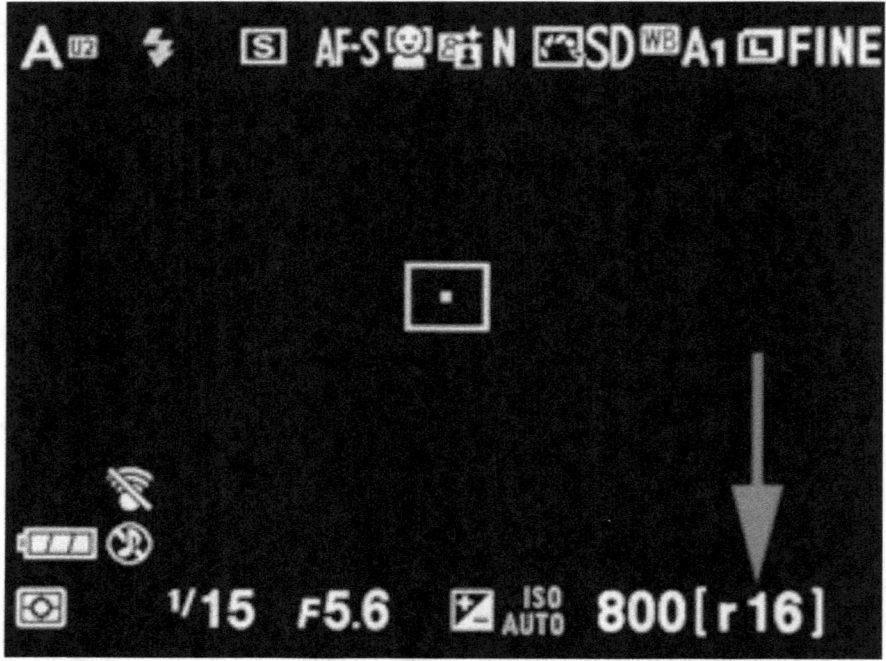

The letter "r" followed by a numerical value will appear in the lower right corner of the Live view screen as the shutter-release button is held down. The value denotes the estimated quantity of images that can be stored in the memory reservoir of the camera prior to a reduction in the frame rate. When the camera is in JPEG fine mode, the value r16 indicates that 16 additional FINE JPEG images can be stored in the internal memory buffer before it is complete.

The camera will continue to capture images even if the internal memory buffer is full, however, so long as the shutter-release button is depressed. However, it will be unable to maintain the 4 fps rate and will only take another image after the one in the buffer has been written to the memory card.

RAW mode restricts the number of frames that can be captured before the buffer is filled to nine. The camera has a maximum output of 26 frames per second in JPEG mode, with the exception of the greater compression modes (JPEG normal or JPEG basic), when it depletes its buffer memory and the frame rate decelerates to keep up.

Self-Timer Release Mode

The Self-timer enables one to capture images without touching the camera physically.

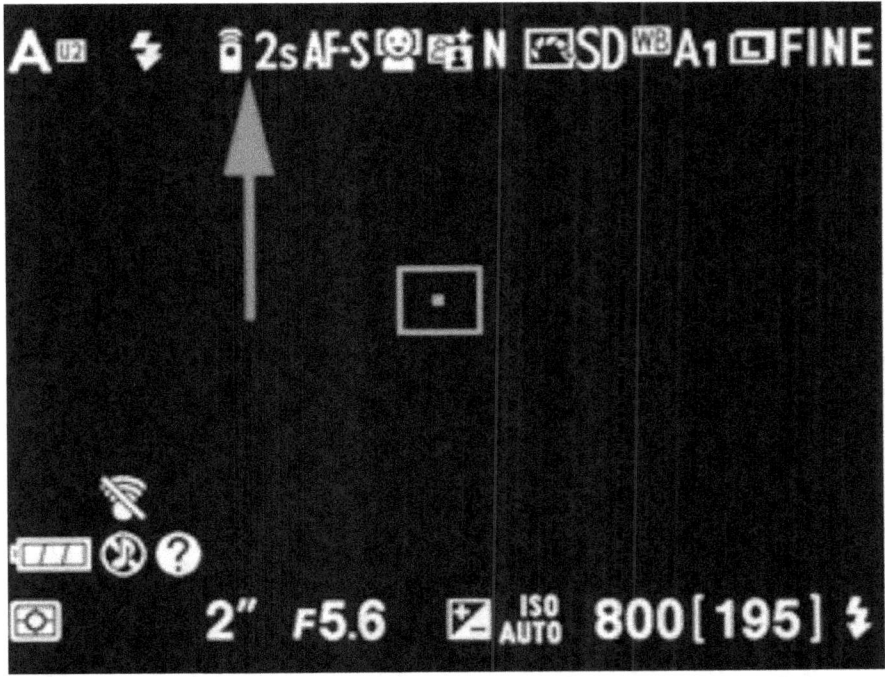

This mode features a modifiable countdown time which elapses before the shutter release is automatically pressed by the self-timer. By default, the Self-timer is set to expire in ten seconds (10 s). But you can delay the time-out by selecting Self-timer from the Setup Menu; options include 2, 5, 10, or 20 seconds.

Additionally, the number of photos captured during each countdown cycle can be modified via the Setup Menu > Self-timer > Number of shots (ranging from one to nine photographs).

You can enable the beep-beep-beep sound when the Self-timer is counting down the seconds until the shutter button is released via the Setup Menu > Beep.

Delayed Remote (ML-L3) Release Mode

Utilizing the delayed remote (ML-L3) Release mode with the Nikon ML-L3 infrared remote control is possible.

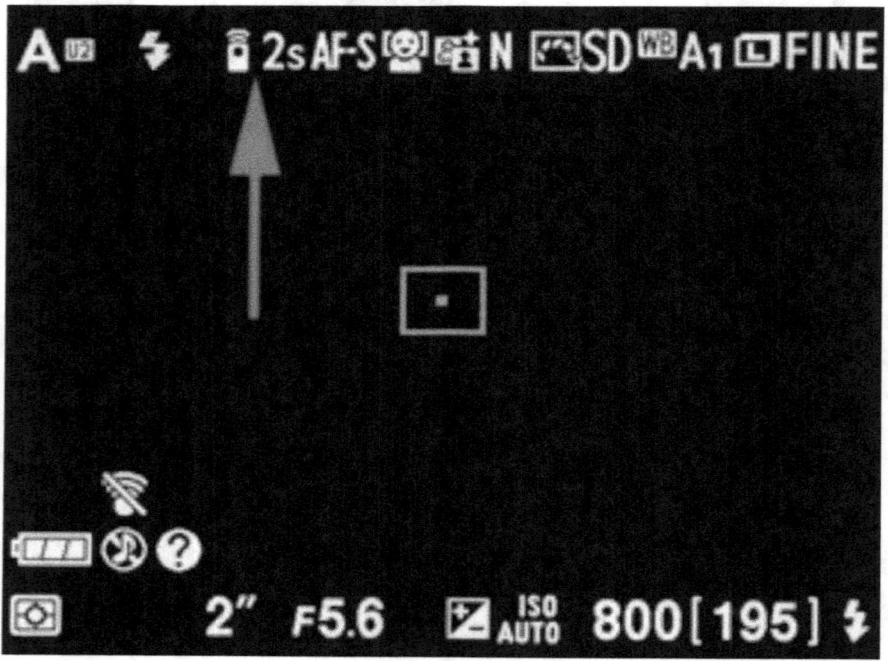

To initiate the autofocus process in this mode, press the release button midway on the ML-L3. In order to capture an image, hold down the shutter completely. The shutter will thereafter be released after two seconds have passed.

Quick-Response (ML-L3) Release Mode

The operation of Quick-response (ML-L3) Release mode is comparable to that of Delayed remote (ML-L3) Release mode, with the exception that the shutter is activated immediately. Also, the camera can be fired remotely, devoid of any cables or connections.

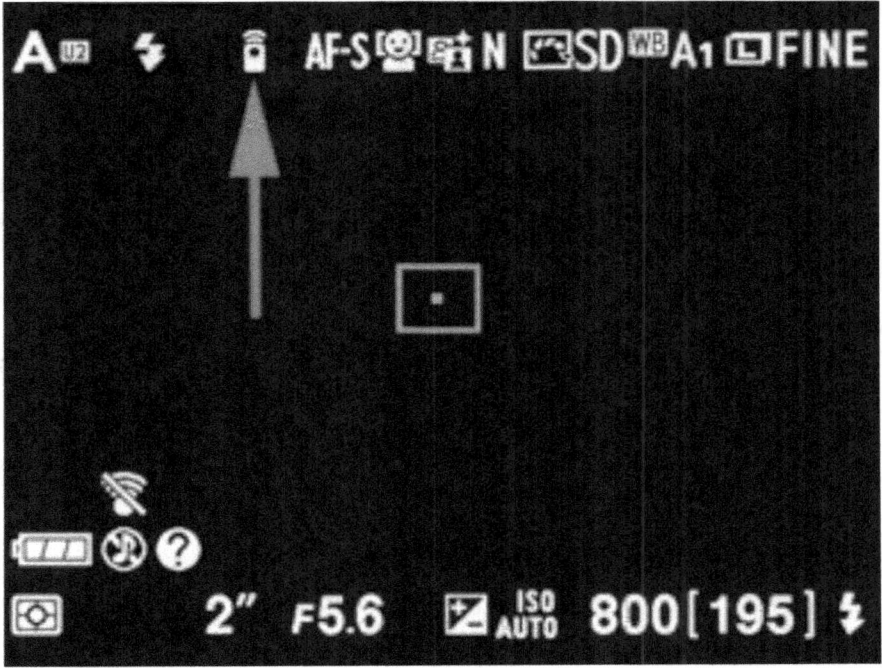

To initiate the autofocus process in this mode, press the release button midway on the ML-L3. In order to capture an image, press the shutter button completely. Thereafter, the shutter will be initiated promptly by the camera.

Movie Recording Release Mode

Utilizing this mode is the only way the camera can be set to video mode.

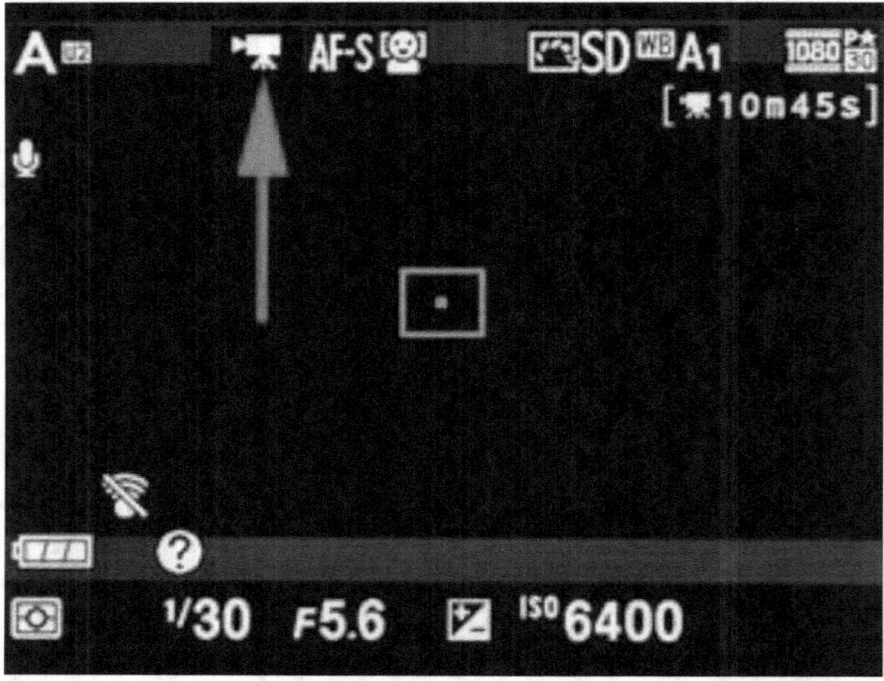

Note; After selecting this mode, the camera has no additional external controls for video capture, with the exception of the shutter-release button, which is used to initiate and terminate the video.

METERING

The exposure in the Nikon camera is determined by a meter, which examines a broad area of the frame in a flexible manner in order to deliver an accurate reading.

The camera can determine the exposure using matrix metering in accordance with the distribution of color, distance, luminance, and composition. The majority of individuals who leave the light meter on Matrix achieve outstanding results. Some individuals continue to utilize center-weighted metering due to their familiarity with this more traditional form of light meter. When metering a very small area of the frame for more precise subject exposures in challenging lighting conditions, the spot meter is of great assistance. To modify the metering mode, perform the subsecuent procedures:

1. From the Quick Menu, select Metering by pressing the i icon, then press the OK button.

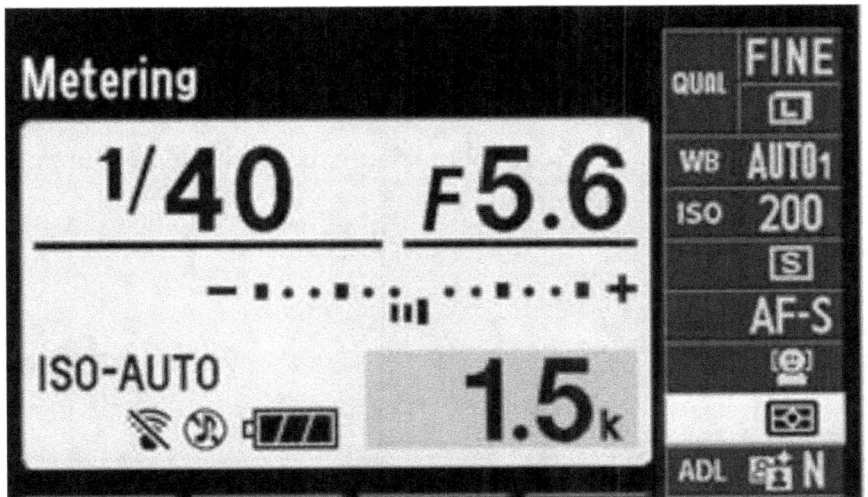

2. From the menu, choose one of the three meter modes. Note; on the Quick Menu screen, the name of the meter type will appear above the small image.

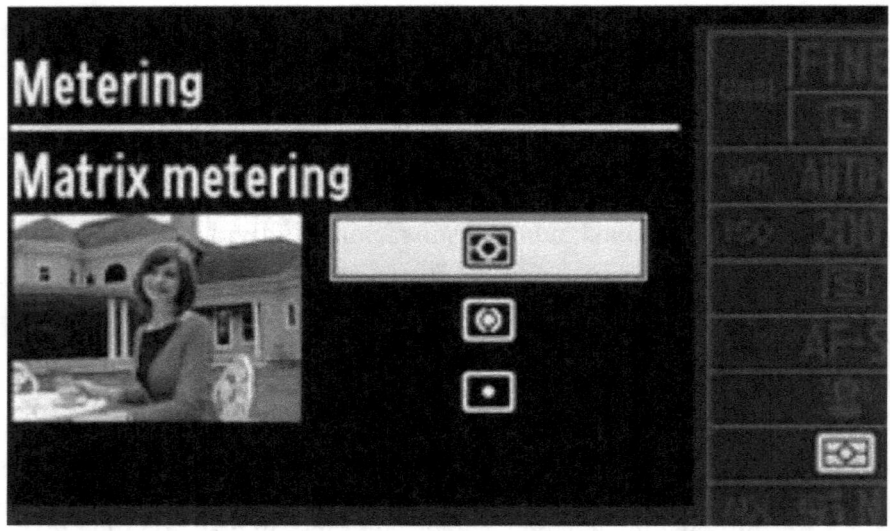

3. Select the meter by pressing down the OK button.

Matrix Metering

The color matrix metering system on the Nikon camera is among the most versatile and potent automatic exposure meters currently available in compact cameras.

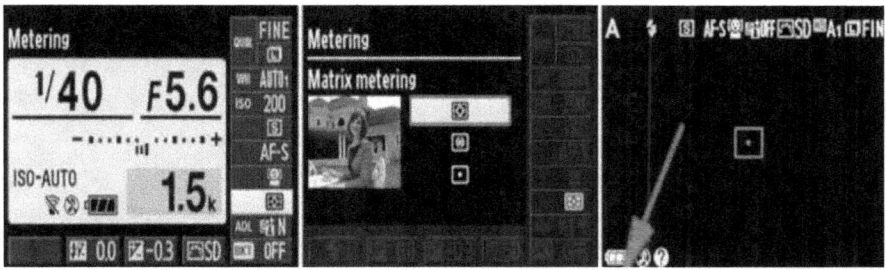

For those curious as to how matrix metering operates, the camera stores characteristics for tens of thousands of images in the form of intricate mathematical formulas. In conjunction with sophisticated evaluative computations and proprietary Nikon software, these attributes are utilized to assess the image displayed on the monitor. The meter is subsequently adjusted to ensure that the majority of your images have accurate exposures.

A simple example is when the horizon traverses the central region of an image. As opposed to the brilliant sky above, the earth below is considerably subdued. After comparing this image to hundreds of comparable images in the camera's database, the metering system selects and inputs a meter setting automatically.

Each image is evaluated in four critical areas by the meter. By comparing the luminance levels across different regions of the scene, it is possible to ascertain the overall range of EV values. It subsequently observes the subject's and environment's color. It also determines the distance to the subject by determining how far away the lens is focused. Additionally, the compositional elements of the subject are examined. After acquiring this information, the meter proceeds to analyze hundreds of image attributes stored in the camera's database, performs intricate calculations, and generates an

83

exposure value that is typically accurate, even when confronted with complex illumination conditions.

Center-Weighted Metering

You have the ability to convert the exposure meter on the camera into a center-weighted meter with a weighting that is adjustable in size.

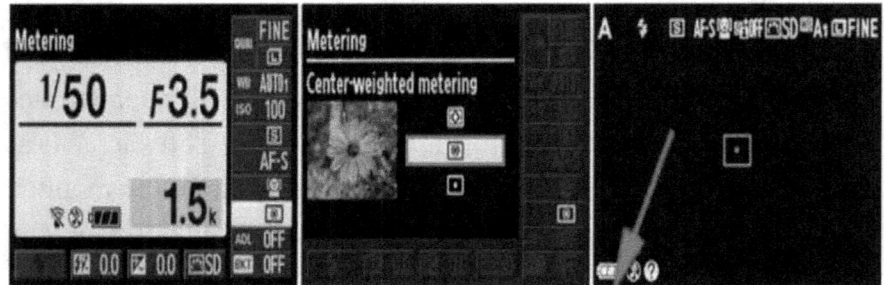

Although the Center-weighted meter in the camera measures the entire frame, it allocates 75% of its readings to an invisible circle located in the frame's center. The remaining twenty-five percent of the frame beyond the circle is utilized for the remaining metering.

Spot Metering

Generally, a spot meter is sufficient for taking any kind of photo. For example, when obtaining precise exposure measurements for a minute portion of the frame or when obtaining multiple meter readings from different small areas, the camera can be modified to the spot metering, to suit your choice. The Spot Meter measures the minute area of the movable focusing rectangle that is shown on the camera screen.

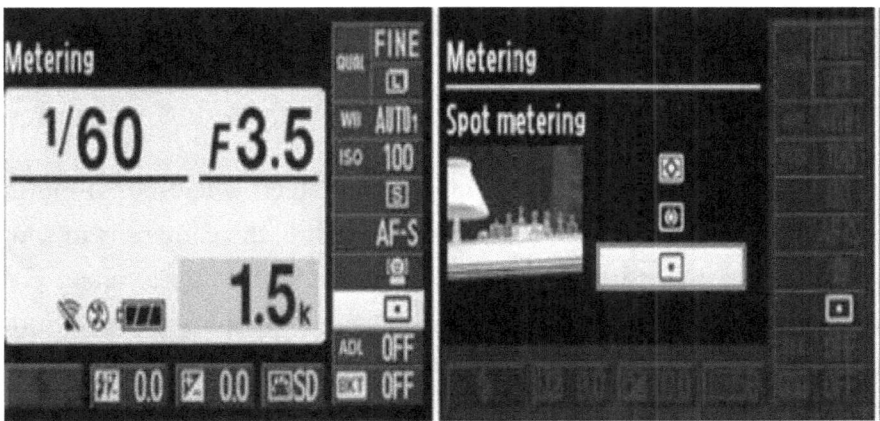

The Spot meter of the camera is denoted by a small circle encircling the autofocus location.

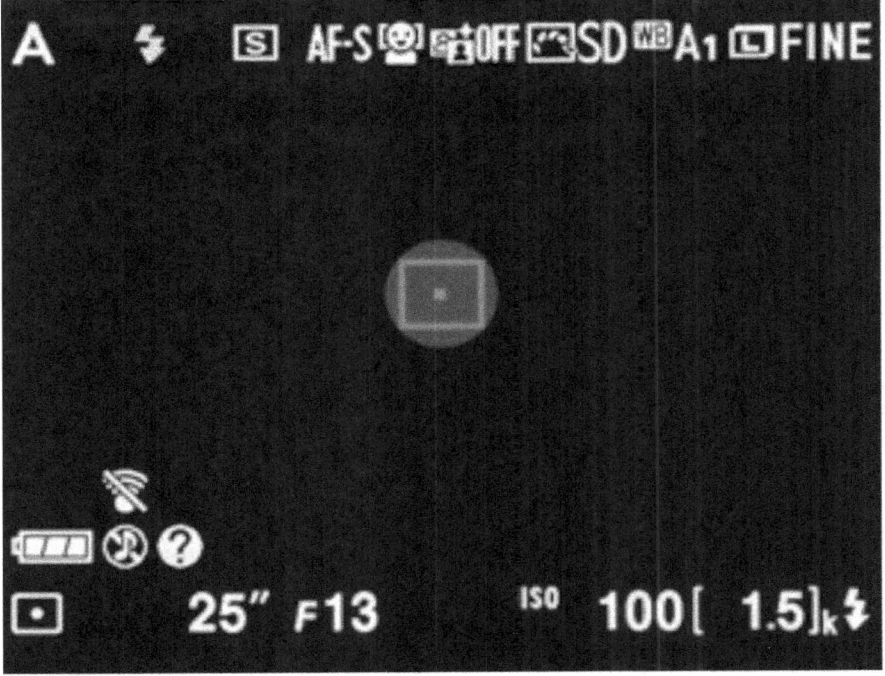

It scarcely encircles the monitor's AF pointer area. As the spot meter tracks the AF point around the monitor, it is possible to move the spot around the frame by rotating the multi selector and setting your meter.

Obtaining an accurate spot reading is guaranteed when the AF point is moved to a small section of the subject while the camera is in spot meter mode. Indeed, it is possible to ascertain an approximate EV range of light values across the entire image by employing your Spot meter and contrasting multiple manual spot readings. If the values surpass eight to nine EV stops, you will be required to determine the most critical component of the subject and meter accordingly.

Generally, unconcerned weather conditions prevail on overcast days, as the sensor's recording capabilities typically encompass a sufficient spectrum of light values. During periods of intense sunlight, the spectrum of light that the sensor is capable of capturing can be doubled. Hence, keep in mind that spot metering frequently involves a compromise. One may possess the capability to precisely expose a specific region of an image with extreme specificity, or alternatively, employ the Zone System, which involves averaging multiple manual readings to obtain the appropriate exposure across the entire frame. The decision is at your discretion, contingent upon the specific shooting circumstances.

When utilizing a spot meter to measure the shadows cast by a fair-skinned individual standing in direct sunlight, the shadows may yield minimal or negligible data. They will appear extremely dark and underexposed. When metering from the shadows, the individual's face will likely appear predominantly white.

Note; spot metering is recommended to obtain precise meter measurements of tiny areas surrounding the subject. Keep in mind that the Spot meter only evaluates the small area it detects, so it is unable to adjust the camera for anything other than that one minuscule area. Although spot metering demands some skill, it is an extremely professional method of exposing photographs.

EXPOSURE MODES

The Coolpix 950 is a P, S, A, and M camera. That is the abbreviated sequence of primary photography modes that grant you manual control over the aperture and shutter speed of the camera. Furthermore, the camera is equipped with an AUTO mode, which allows you to capture high-quality images without concern for exposure, and 19 scene modes.

The camera features a single control for activating the AUTO, SCENE, P, S, A, M, U1, and U2 modes. This control is often referred to as the Mode dial.

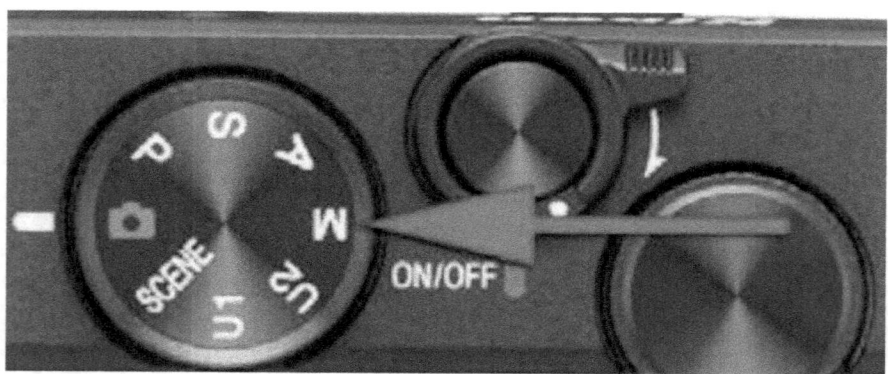

Let's examine each mode of exposure in depth.

Programmed Auto (P) Mode

The Programmed auto (P) mode is intended for situations in which you want to take pictures without giving much thought to the camera's settings, but still have the ability to adjust the settings if necessary. The camera autonomously determines the optimal shutter speed, aperture, and exposure meter to produce high-quality images, eliminating the need for manual adjustment. In this mode, aperture override is possible through the use of the Command dial.

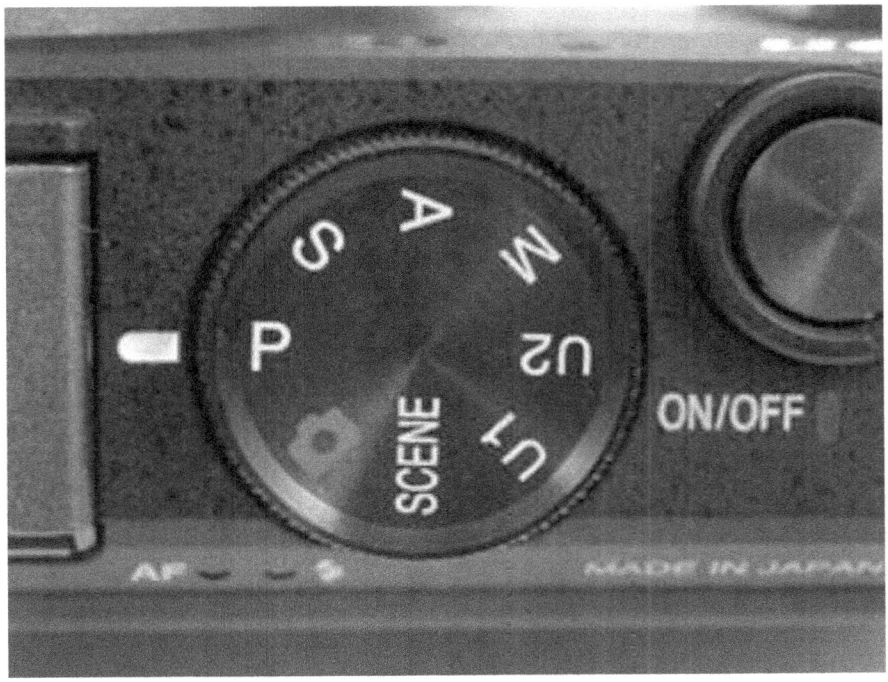

Programmed auto is a useful setting to activate when you wish to delegate aperture and shutter speed control to the camera while maintaining control over the light. It is similar to AUTO mode, with the exception that you determine when to use the pop-up speedlight as opposed to the camera doing so. It also provides an emergency aperture override function. If you require a greater depth of field, you might opt for a smaller aperture. You can accomplish this by rotating the Command dial on the camera, after which, you will have control over the aperture, while the camera manages the shutter.

Additionally, P mode consists of two components: Programmed Auto and Flexible Program. The Flexible program mode functions in the same way as Aperture-Priority auto (A) mode. In Flexible program mode, only the aperture is under your control; the camera is responsible for regulating the shutter speed. As the Command dial is rotated in a clockwise direction, the aperture is reduced. Invert the device counterclockwise to enlarge the aperture. Nikon only provides aperture control in Flexible program mode; thus, Flexible program mode functions similarly to aperture-priority (A) mode.

Note; in this mode, you must be wary of additional clicks. If you turn the Command dial counterclockwise until the aperture reaches its utmost value (f/2.8), it causes the camera to begin to count clicks without performing any additional actions. However, to restore aperture movement, you must retract the dial by the equivalent number of clicks, which can reach a maximum of 15 clicks.

Shutter-Priority Auto (S) Mode

When you need to adjust the shutter speed while the camera maintains the optimal aperture for the available light, use the shutter-priority auto function. To activate this mode, modify the shutter speed via the Command dial while the aperture is controlled by the camera.

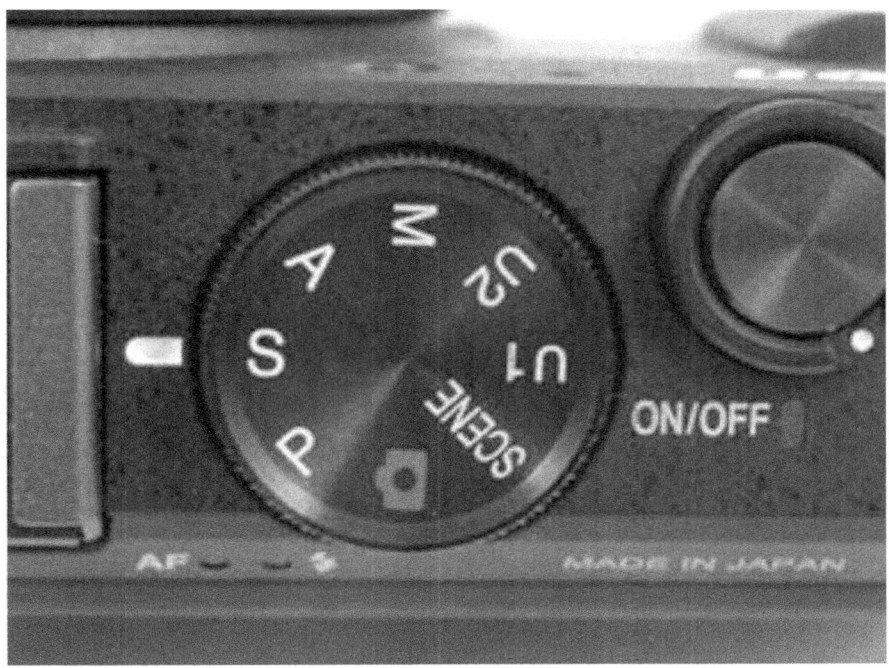

Note; Events like, sports, air shows, auto races, and other fast-moving subjects, all warrant meticulous shutter speed management. When photographing an in-flight bird, it is advisable to employ a shutter speed that permits a minimal amount of motion distortion in the wings without completely capturing the body of the bird.

There are instances when slow shutter speed settings are desirable for time exposures or special effects, such as photographing a picturesque autumn stream featuring a small cascade. Simply rotate the Command dial to any value between 30 seconds and 1/2000 second to alter the shutter speed. For slower shutter speeds, rotate the dial counterclockwise; for higher shutter speeds, rotate it clockwise. Aperture adjustment is performed automatically by the camera to ensure proper exposure.

Caution is advised when the shutter speed is decreased to 1/125 second. Many individuals encounter difficulties with camera motion at 1/60 second and below. One can likely achieve precise images in the time range of 1/60 to 1/15 second by maintaining a still position, bracing arms against the torso, and placing one foot in front of the other with the other.

Aperture-Priority Auto (A) Mode

People who are interested in meticulously manipulating the depth of field, including nature and macro photographers, frequently operate their cameras in aperture-priority auto (A) mode.

For optimal exposures, aperture-priority auto (A) mode permits you to adjust the aperture while the camera handles the shutter speed. To adjust the aperture, you need to modify the Command dial. For smaller aperture openings, rotate the dial counterclockwise; for larger aperture openings, rotate the dial clockwise. The camera has a minimum aperture of f/22 and a maximum aperture of f/2.8.

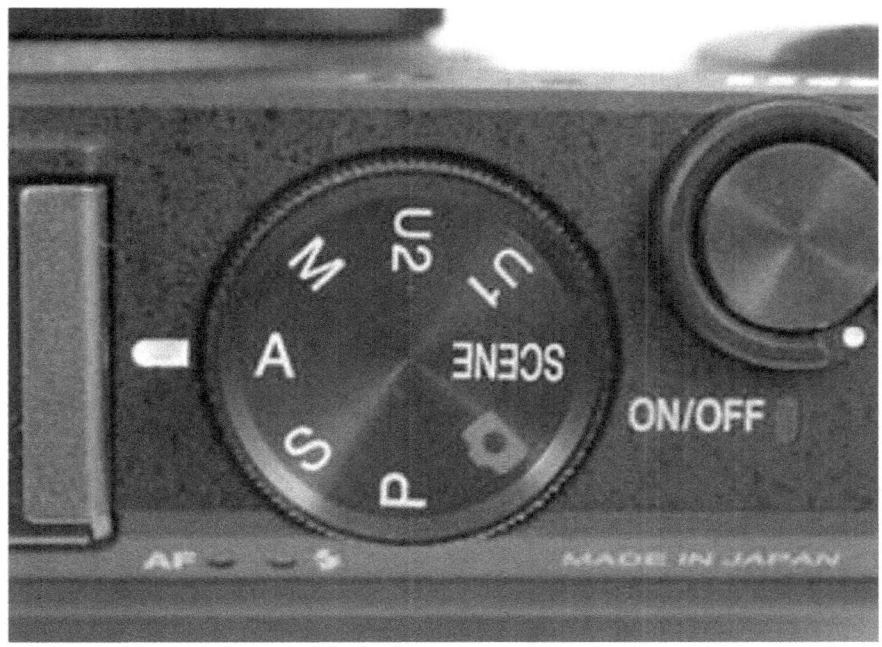

Aperture regulates the depth of field (DOF), also known as the zone of sharpness, of an image in a direct manner. DOF is a fundamental principle that photographers must fully grasp. In essence, it grants you the ability to regulate the depth or range of precise focus in your photographs.

Manual (M) Mode

It provides full control over the aperture, shutter speed, and ISO sensitivity, allowing you to make all exposure decisions despite the light meter's recommendations.

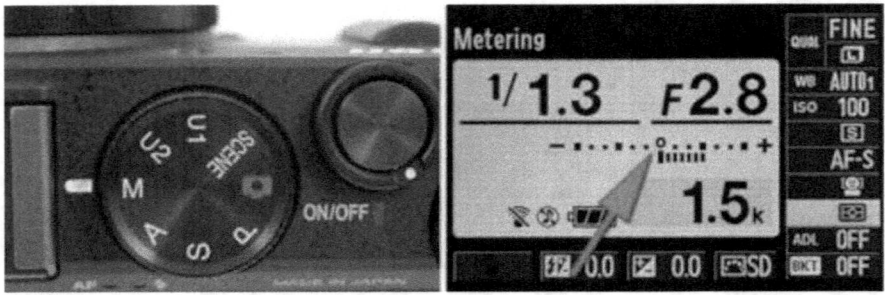

The camera screen shows a plus sign (+) positioned on the right side and a minus sign (-) on the left side when the camera is set to Manual Mode. A bar will appear beneath the analog exposure display while the subject is being metered. It will extend from the zero point in the center toward the plus side to signify overexposure, or toward the minus side to signify underexposure. The degree of overexposure or underexposure can be determined by counting the points and lines that the bar traverses as it approaches either extreme. The objective is to have no data points visible beyond the zero point on the exposure indicator scale.

In this mode, aperture adjustment is possible via the Multi Selector, while shutter speed modification is accomplished via the Command dial. Hence, in Manual mode, the aperture (used to control depth of field) and shutter speed (used to control motion) can be adjusted. Note; reduce the aperture if the image requires a little more depth of field; however, be mindful to decelerate the shutter speed; otherwise, the image might be underexposed. If the need arises unexpectedly for a quicker shutter speed, adjust the shutter speed while compensating by widening the aperture.

It should be noted that the user possesses full authority over the camera and is responsible for determining the shutter speed and aperture under this mode, and although the camera meter provides recommendations, the last decision on the exposure rests with the subject. Manual mode encourages deliberate and enjoyable photography. It provides users with the most control over how their image turns out to be. Lastly, if you want to know how to correctly set your exposures, you need to practice more.

Auto Exposure Mode

Auto exposure is utilized when capturing an image without being bothered about what the camera does. In Auto mode, the only factors that require attention are the composition of the image and the state of charge of the battery.

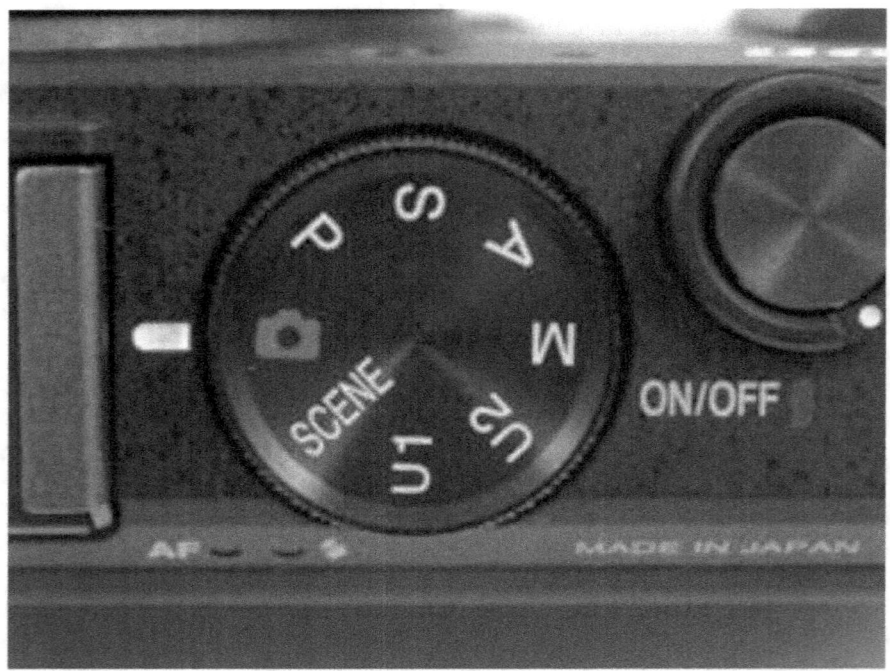

Many of the internal modes of the camera become completely automatic when Auto is engaged; they cannot be adjusted. For example, the following critical camera functions are activated automatically when the Auto setting is chosen on the Mode dial:

- "White balance

- AF-area mode

- Metering mode

- Active D-Lighting

- Picture Control

- Exposure and flash compensation

- Built-in Speedlight flash"

Effectively, what you do in this mode is that you surrender control over the camera's functions in exchange for the assurance that a quality image will be produced by the camera. Hence, in most situations, selecting Auto will result in the camera producing images of its usual high quality. However, the camera may increase the ISO sensitivity and Active D-Lighting in challenging conditions in order to capture an image, even if doing so compromises image quality.

Scene Modes

Nikon classifies scene modes as "creative photography" modes. They enable novice photographers to access the camera settings that they would likely employ with greater expertise. These modes enable you to consistently produce high-quality images; as your expertise develops, you can subsequently employ the P, S, A, and M modes to exert greater artistic autonomy over your images.

When opting to utilize scene modes, do so with the knowledge that you may eventually acquire the ability to manipulate the image with greater precision using the P, S, A, and M modes. Nikon has endowed the Mode dial with the P, S, A, M, Auto, and Scene modes, thereby granting users the ability to operate the camera with a combination of complete manual control and partial or full automation.

The Nikon camera features nineteen unique scene modes that are intended to grant novice photographers the ability to manipulate specific photographic styles. After reviewing a list of the different scene modes, we will analyze each one in greater depth.

- "Portrait

- Landscape

- Child

- Sports

- Close up

- Night portrait

- Night landscape

- Party/indoor

- Beach/snow

- Sunset

- Dusk/dawn

- Pet portrait

- Candlelight

- Blossom

- Autumn colors

- Food

- Silhouette

- High key

- Low key"

Proceed as follows to choose a scene mode:

1. Choose "Scene" on the Mode dial atop the camera.

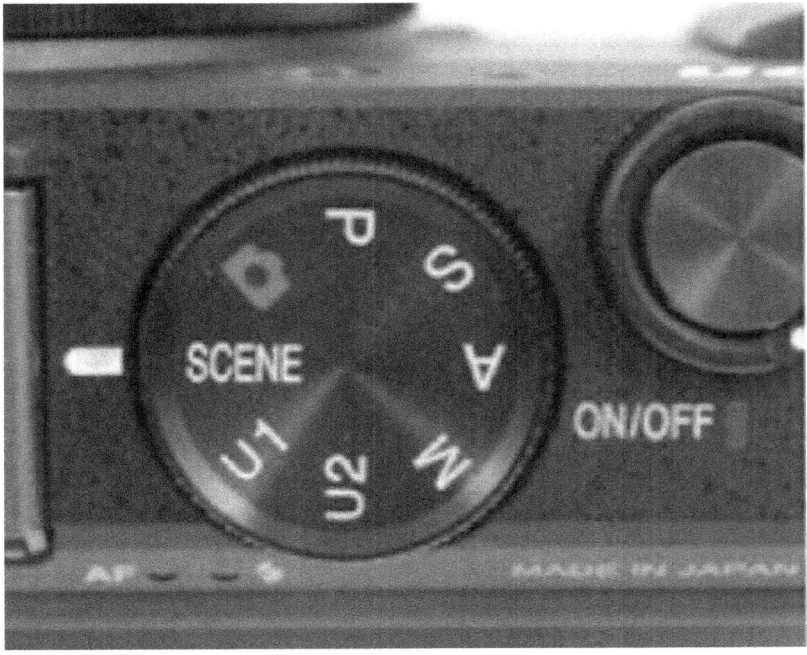

2. Rotate the Command dial while looking at the monitor to see the different mode options.

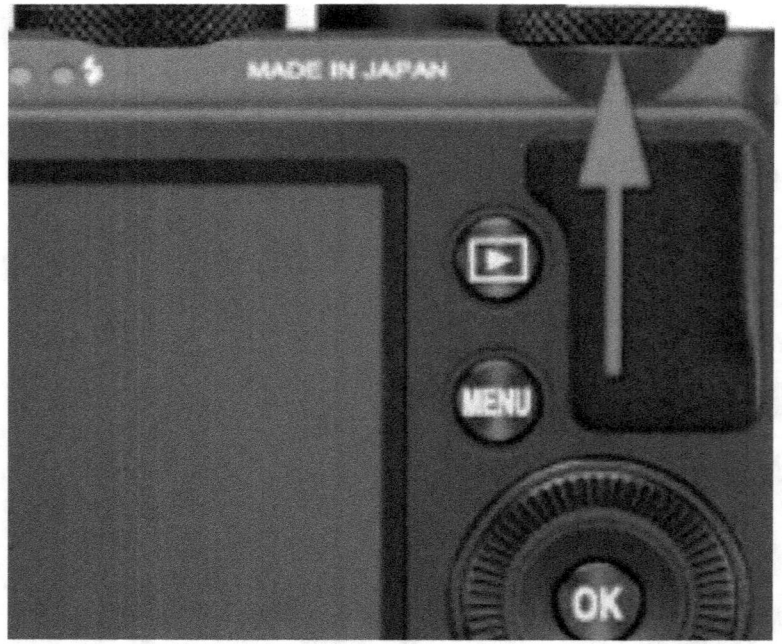

3. At the upper left corner of the display, a graphical representation of the edge of a dial with symbols attached, will be displayed.

   Each rotation of the Command dial corresponds to a distinct Scene mode, denoted on the screen by a small icon accompanied by an illustrative word. The monitor enters Scene mode for approximately four seconds prior to turning off. Continue to rotate the Command dial to access additional Scene modes.

4. Pause for four seconds after selecting the desired Scene mode before the Live view screen appears.

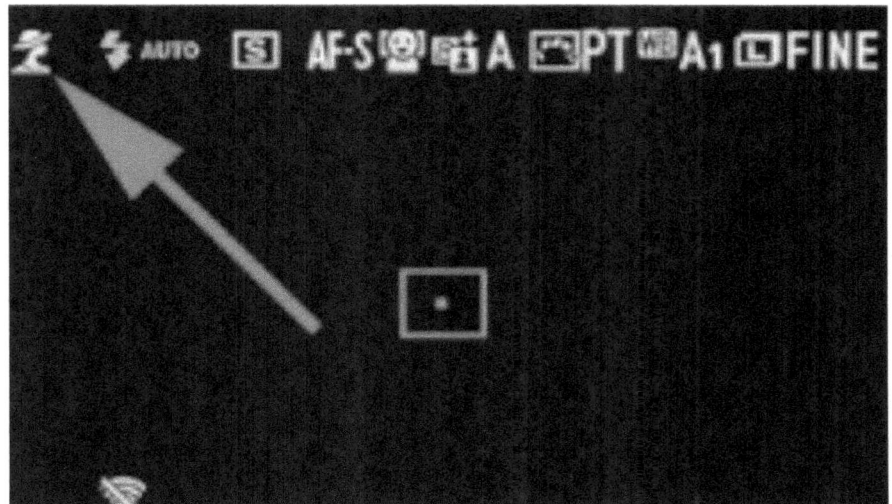

Scene is denoted by the word Scene at the bottom of the display and a symbol in the upper-left corner of the display. At this point you can take photographs using the scene mode you have selected.

Currently, we will examine the scene modes. In each of the subsequent nineteen sections.

Scene Mode for Portrait

When shooting portraits or still subjects, use the portrait scene mode. The symbol for Portrait Mode resembles a woman with a cap on.

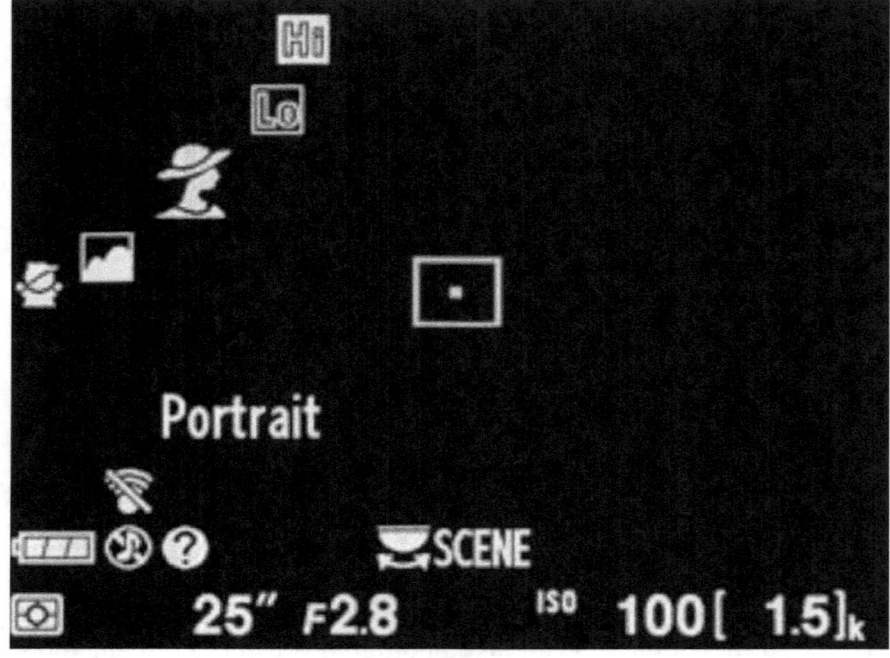

Large apertures and a narrow depth of field are often used by the camera in this mode, bringing the subject into sharp focus and creating a pleasing effect of minimizing background blur. Use this option for capturing images of yourself and a friend or a small group of people. Note, this mode makes color adjustments to highlight good skin tones.

Scene Mode for Landscape

Use the Landscape scene mode, for instance, if you want to shoot places like the mountains. The landscape symbol is represented by two mountain peaks surrounded by a square.

102

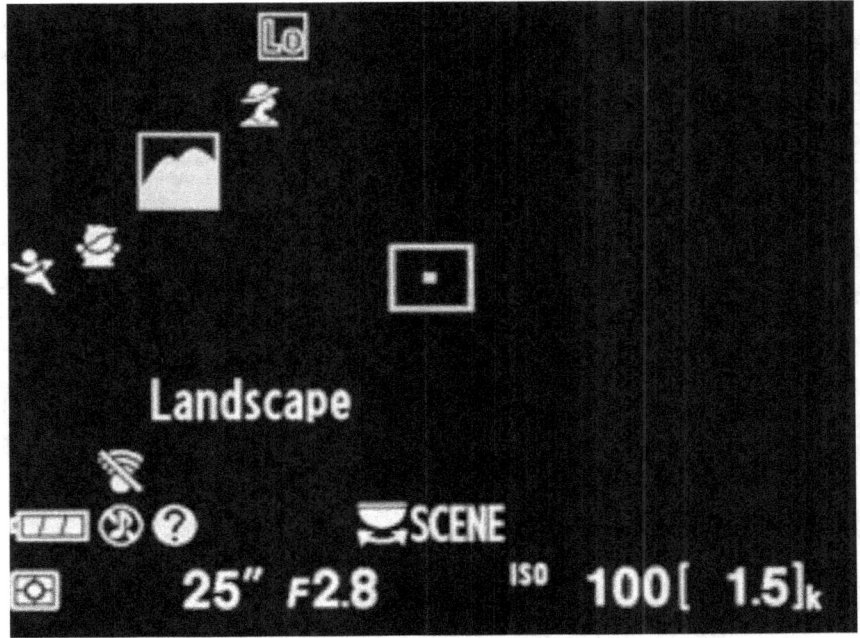

In order to capture the full picturesque scene in crisp detail, it is typically ideal to take landscape photos with a tripod and small aperture. Smaller apertures should also be used in the Landscape mode to increase depth of field. This is similar to utilizing Aperture-priority auto (A) mode, however because the camera selects the aperture, you have less control.

Scene Mode for Children

Child scene mode aims to avoid oversaturating skin tones while balancing the need for vibrant colors in children's clothing and any bright surroundings. Its logo is a picture of a young boy with his arms up and wearing a hat.

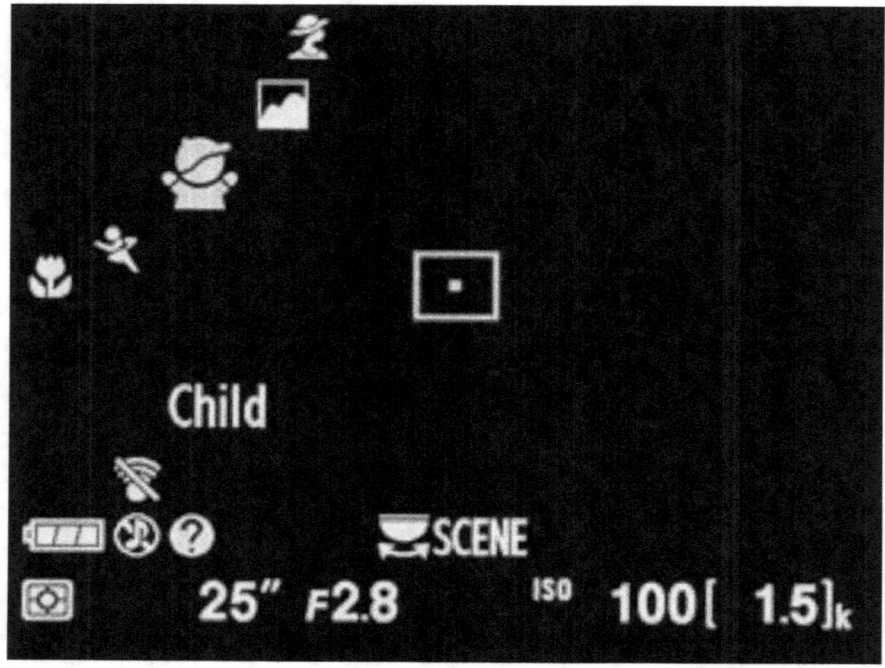

Making skin tones look decent seems to be the main focus of this setting, which also provides you with a tiny enough aperture to have some depth of field and a fast enough shutter speed to record a moving baby. In terms of aperture and shutter speed, it seems to be a balanced mode.

Scene Mode for Sports

The Sports scene option prioritizes quicker shutter speeds since athletes and other subjects are often moving at a high speed. The symbol for the sport scene mode is a runner.

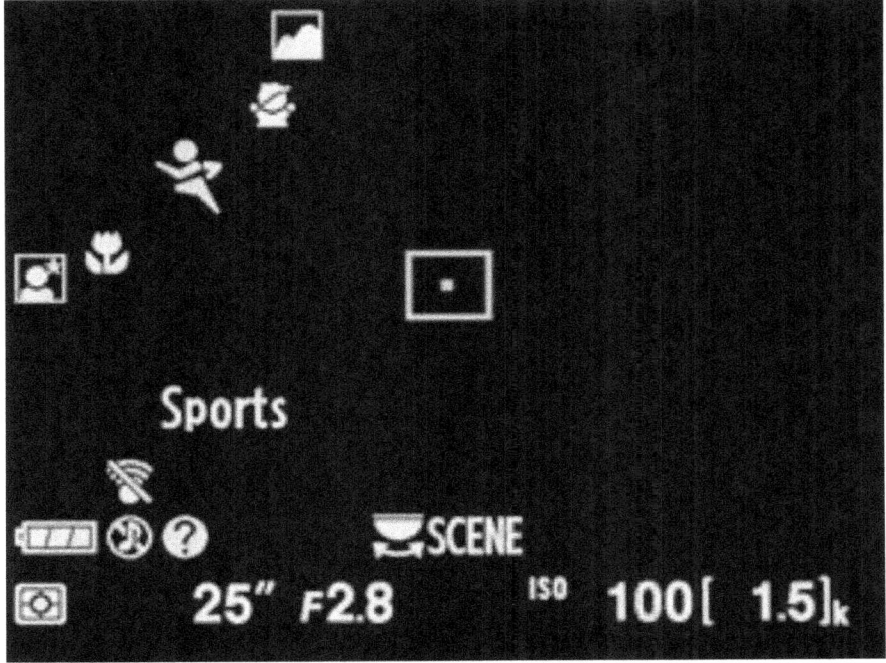

The camera will utilize the quickest shutter speed the light allows and open the aperture to maintain a fair exposure since you don't want sluggish shutter speeds, for instance during an air show or auto race. The Sports scene mode should, however, be used with a short depth of field. Although you have less control over certain shutter speeds, this mode is comparable to utilizing shutter-priority (S) mode.

Scene Mode for shooting Close-Up

Macro mode and blossom mode are other terms for close-up scene mode. A flower is the symbol used to represent the close-up scene mode.

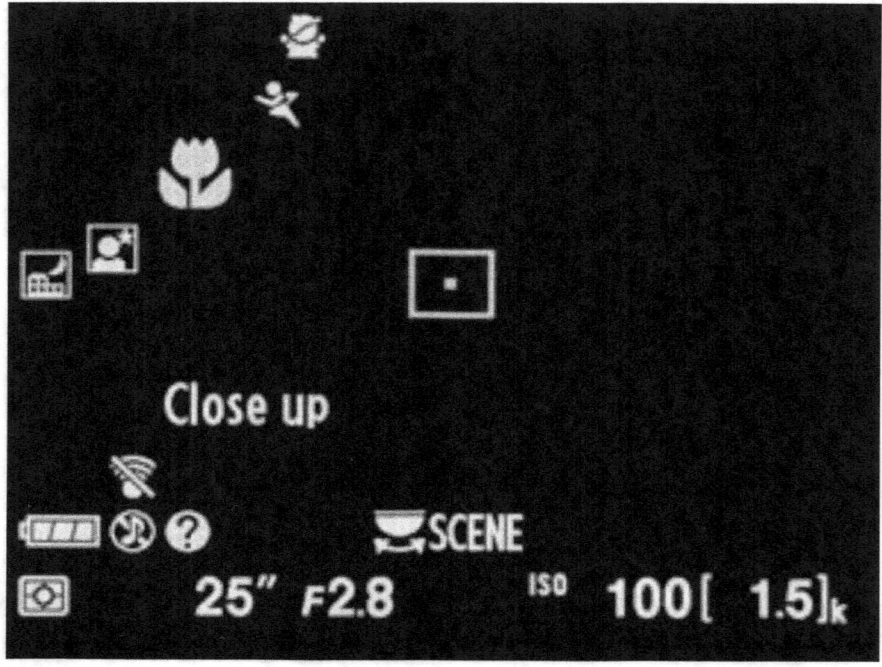

This mode is designed to let you capture up-close shots of little objects like flowers, insects, and other objects. It attempts to strike a compromise between having a shutter speed quick enough to reduce camera vibration and a depth of field deep enough to allow for precise subject focus; this mode seems rather neutral. It functions similarly to the P (programmed auto mode). In this mode, focus is locked on the subject when it has been detected.

Scene Mode for Night Portraits

Similar to close-up scene mode, night portrait mode often employs medium apertures and shutter speeds. Its logo is denoted by a square frame and features a little person with a star on the right side of his head.

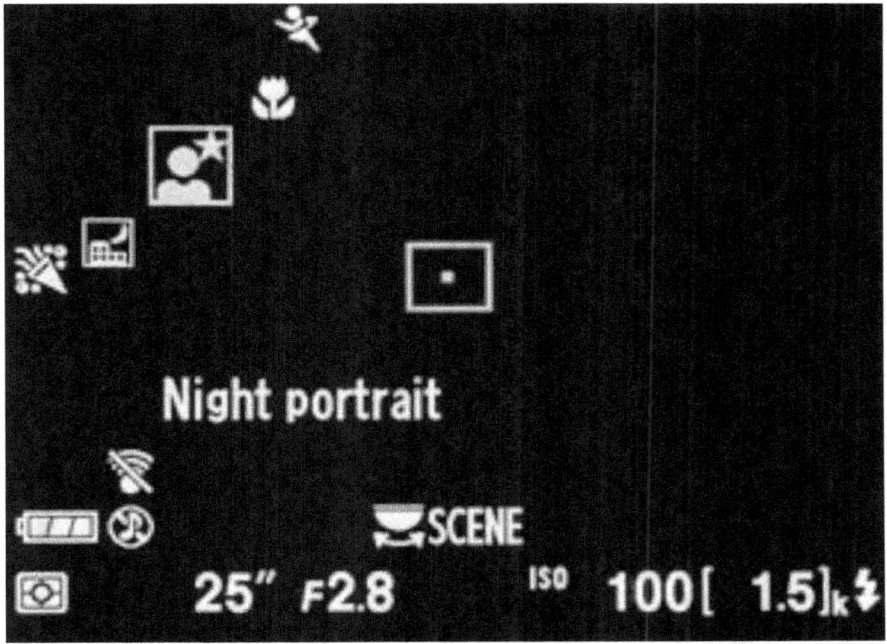

This mode follows this rule: while handheld photography is being done at night, it is advisable to maintain a balance between the shutter speed and aperture. This ensures that the shutter speed remains quick enough to be handled while the aperture remains as wide as possible to allow in the most light. Large apertures seem to be emphasized more so than quick shutter speeds.

Scene Mode for Night Landscape

This setting is intended to be used for nighttime exposures with a tripod. This setting is ideal for taking night time photos of a cityscape or a landscape under the moonlight. The symbol for this mode is a structure with a crescent moon on it.

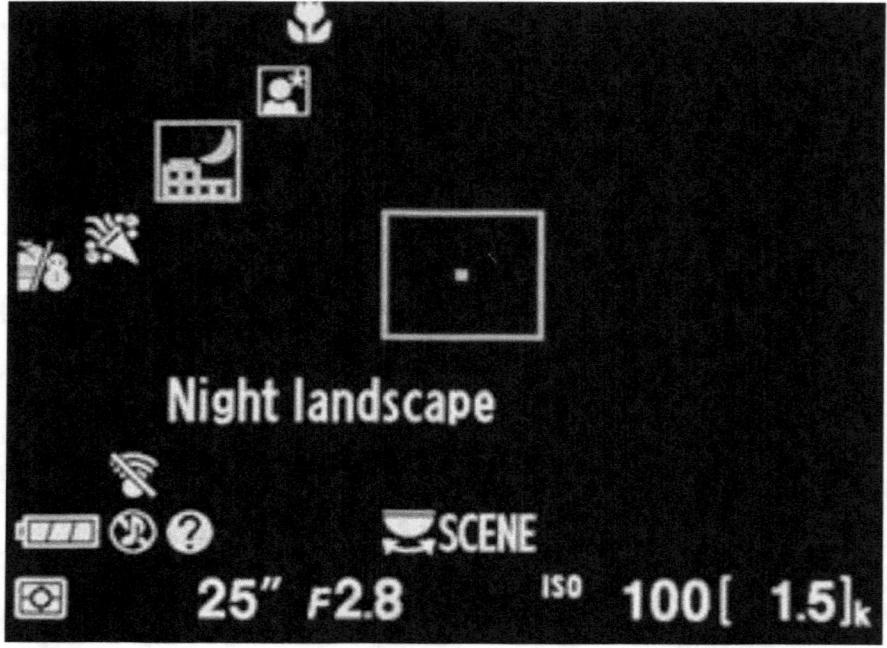

The camera employs noise reduction, longer exposures, and increased ISO sensitivity when it's dark outdoors. According to Nikon, the camera attempts to "reduce unnatural colors" since several light sources have varied colors. However, in this mode the focus assist light and pop-up flash are disabled. If you choose to utilize an accessory shoe-mounted flash for fill light or special effects, the camera will utilize it.

Scene Mode for Indoor Party

Red-eye correction is utilized, and fill flash and ambient background lighting are balanced in the party/indoor scene mode. The symbol for this mode is a little horn with bubbles and confetti.

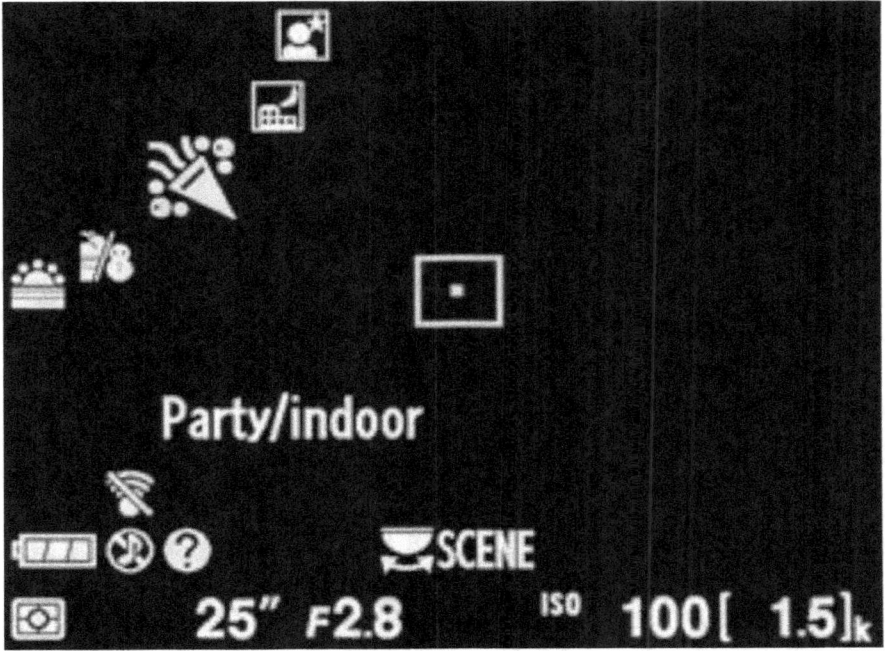

This scene option increases the amount of background light that the sensor detects in an attempt to counteract the appearance of too bright individuals against dark backgrounds. It's excellent for taking pictures of crowds during events. This setting employs slower shutter rates, often about 1/60 second, so be cautious if people are moving fast. If the subject moves too quickly, it might result in ghosting.

Scene Mode for the Beach/Snow

The beach/snow scene style is designed to blend in well with the often sunny stretches of sand, sea, or snow. The symbol for this mode is a snowman in a beach setting.

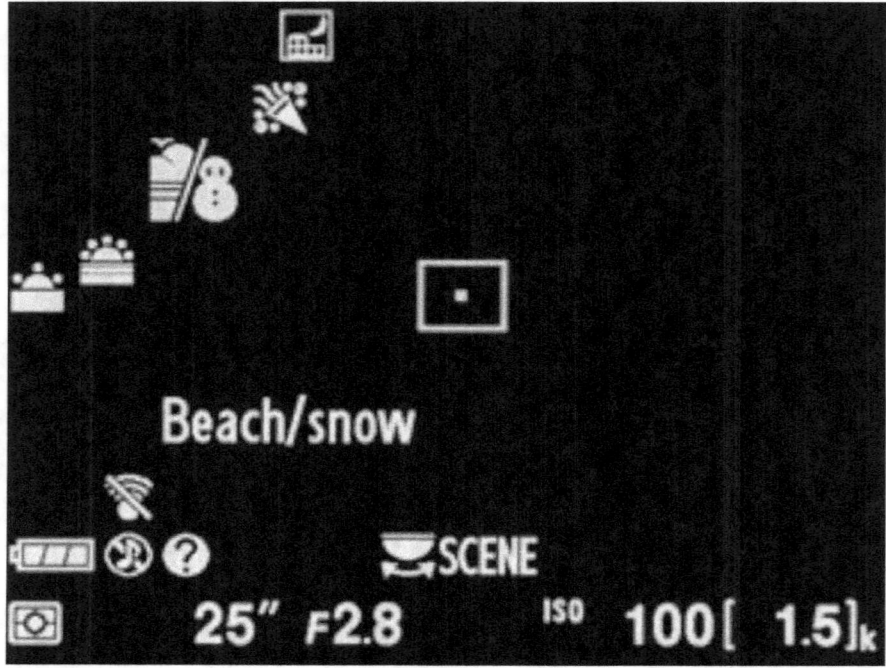

When photographing on a snowy day or while enjoying the beach, choose this setting. Since it's a landscape mode, the picture will be somewhat sharper and the colors will be more intense than usual. In this mode, the focus assist light and pop-up flash are automatically disabled.

Scene Mode for Sunset

The Sunset scene mode is intended to highlight the rich hues that are often seen during sunsets. The symbol for this mode is like a sun that is setting on a horizon.

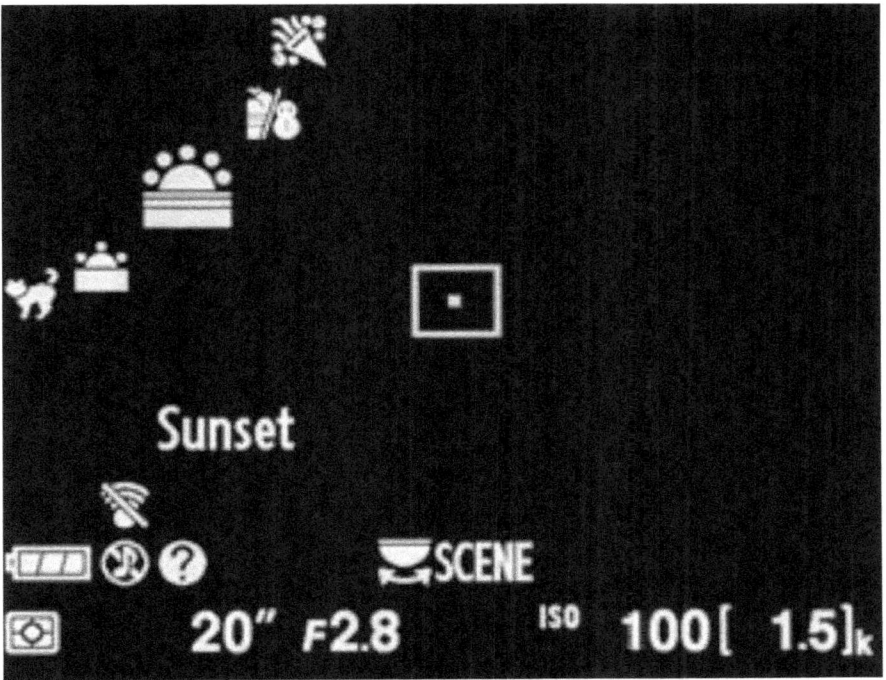

In order to prevent handheld camera motion from obscuring the picture, it would be better to use a tripod while using this setting, which employs narrower apertures and shorter shutter rates. In this mode, the focus assist light and pop-up flash are disabled. However, the camera sharpening intensity is increased in this mode.

The Dawn/Dusk Scene Mode

This mode may over saturate colors, since dusk and dawn often have beautiful color in the sky and subdued hue elsewhere because of darkness. This mode resembles that of the Sun Set Scene Mode, but with lesser sun rays.

111

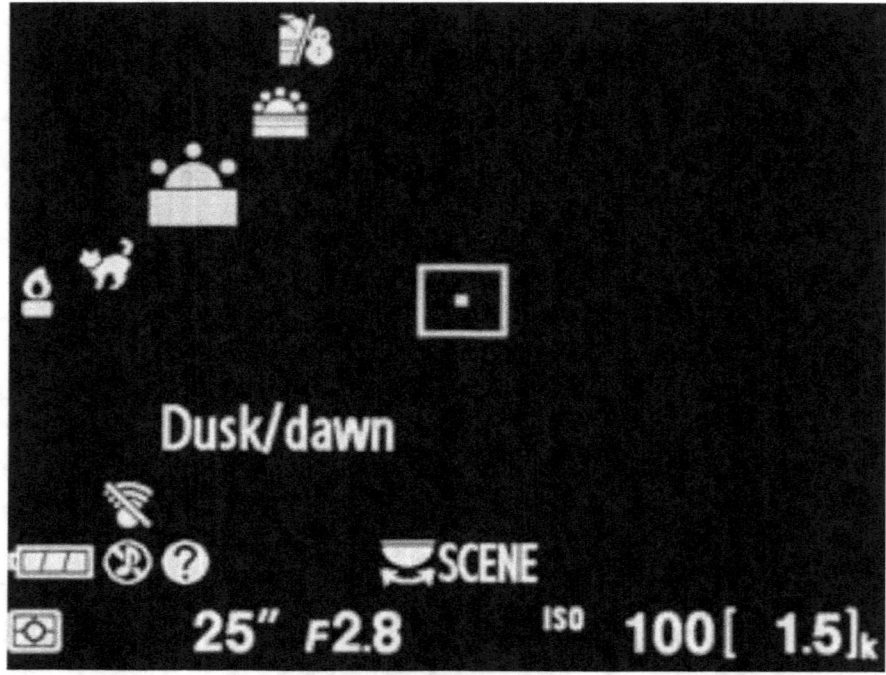

Similar to Sunset mode, this setting employs a colder 4450K white balance. (K is an acronym for Kelvin, a color temperature scale used in color management). It is recommended that you use a tripod in this scene, since the light is so low. In this mode, the focus assist light and pop-up flash are also disabled.

Scene Mode for Pet Portraits

In order to capture events like wriggling kittens and puppies, the pet portrait scene option prioritizes quicker shutter speeds. The symbol of this mode is denoted by a cat image.

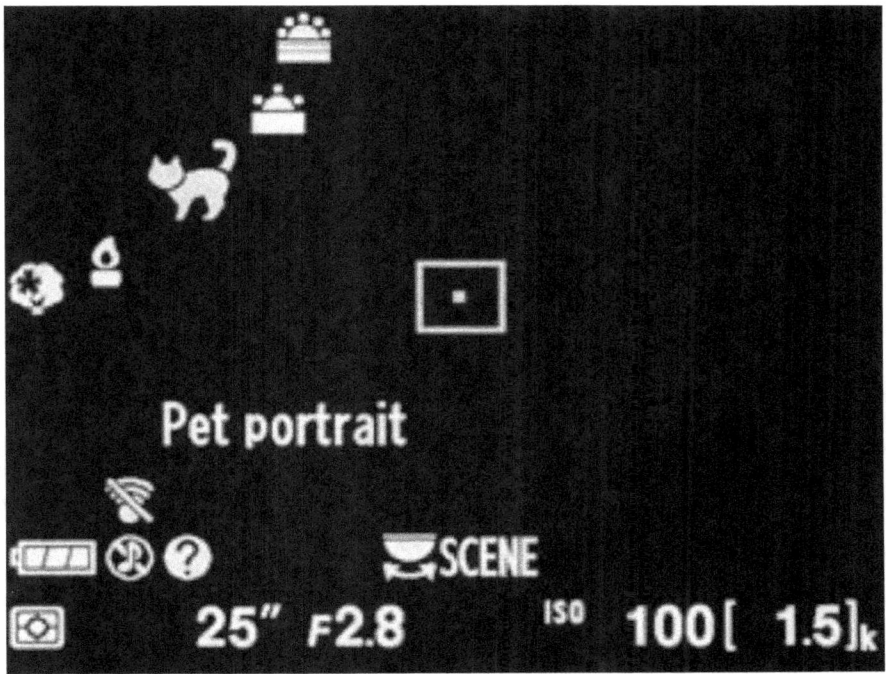

The camera uses a shallow depth of focus to highlight the pet more effectively, when it is set to this mode. Also, the medium settings for color saturation and contrast prevent the pet from having very vibrant hues. However, whether there is a bright backdrop or colored pet clothes, the camera still has the option to boost saturation. Note; to highlight the animal's eyes, fur, beak, feathers, gills, claws, scales, etc. , the camera might also slightly sharpen its exposure.

Scene Mode for Candlelight

This setting is intended for spectacular effects photographs and for taking romantic candlelight photos at events. Its symbol is a candle tip with a flame.

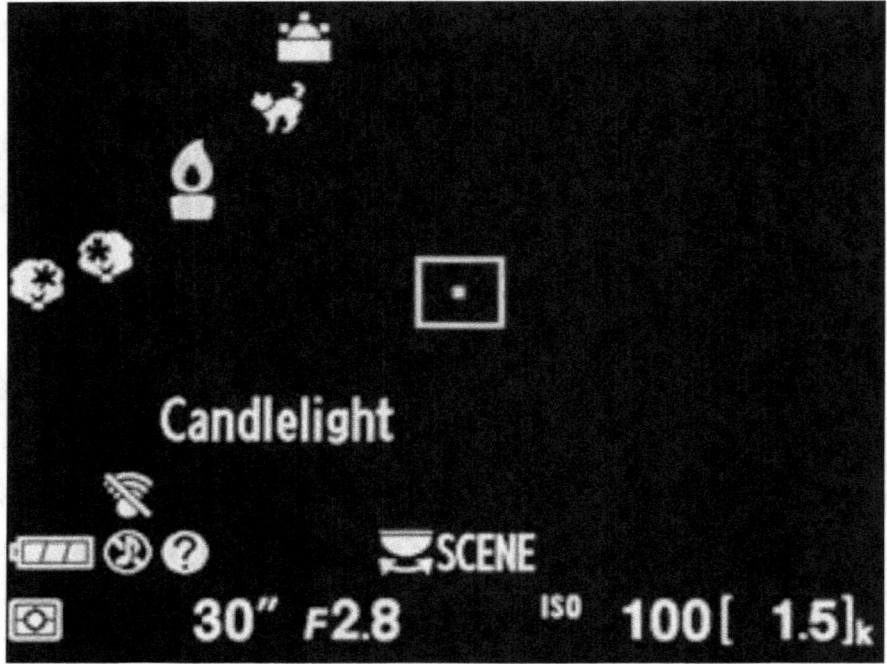

Since the shutter speed in this mode will be sluggish to make up for the low light, if at all possible, utilize a tripod. In this mode, the camera contrasts the warmer hue of candlelight with a medium-cool white balance of 4350K. Note; in the event that you shake the camera in the low ambient light, a little more sharpening will be applied by the camera. There is also no popup flash enabled in this mode. Lastly, the camera locks the subject in place as soon as it acquires a focus.

Blossom Scene Mode

This mode will appeal to you if you visit or are a gardener in an area with an abundance of flowers. It emphasizes color saturation a lot. The symbol of this mode is denoted by a tree with a blossom on the left side.

114

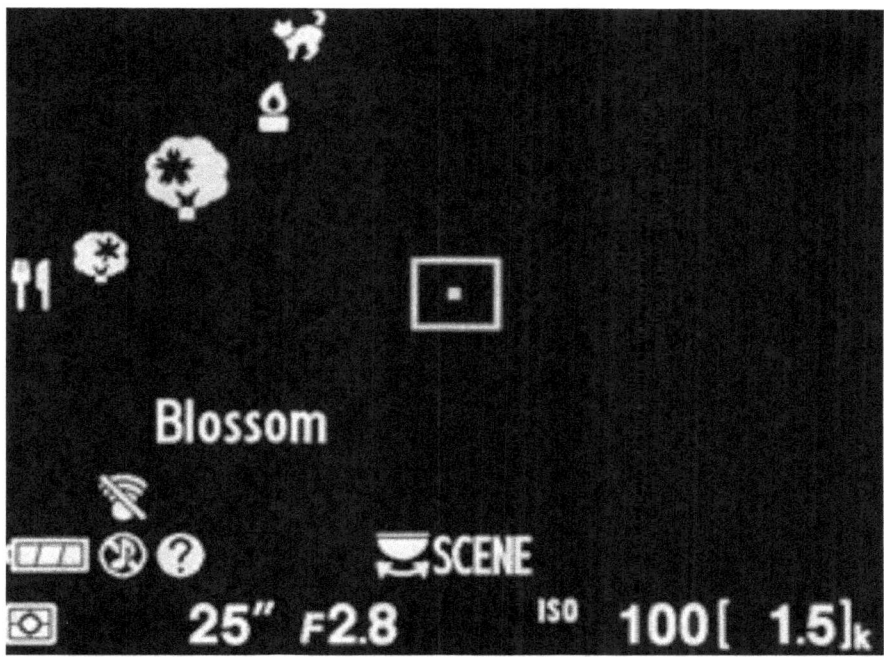

In this mode, the camera utilizes narrower apertures while photographing landscape flower petals because you need a larger depth of field (not closeups). If there is low ambient light while using this mode, use a tripod. Note: There is no popup flash enabled.

Autumn Colors Scene Mode

This mode is represented by an image of a tree with a leaf on the right.

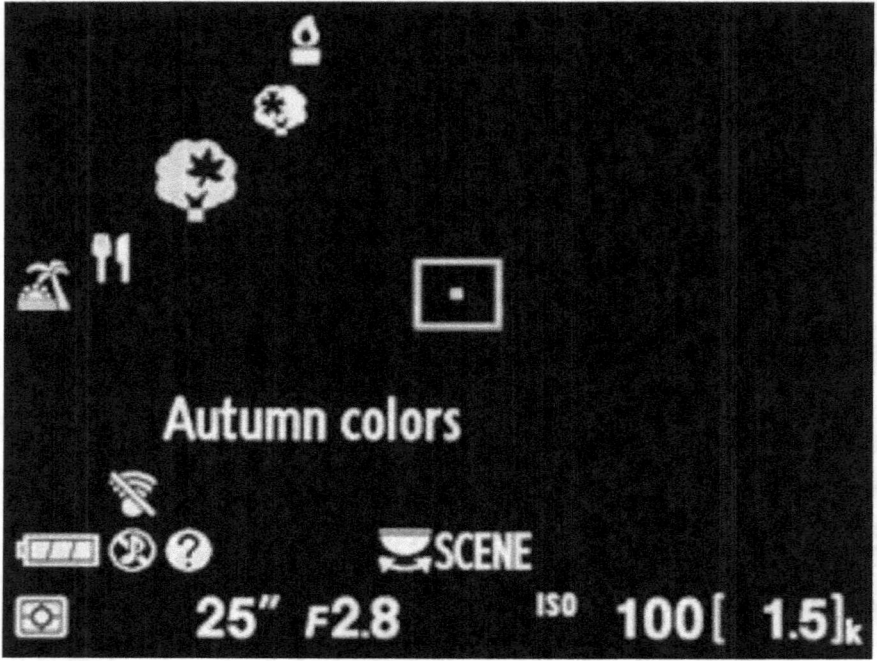

When using this mode, in order to get a deeper depth of focus for those vibrant landscape photographs, the camera employs lower apertures. Use a tripod if there is low light since the shutter speeds will be sluggish in this mode. Note: In this mode, the popup flash is not enabled.

Food Scene Mode

Food photos should be well colored, but not too saturated. Food scene mode gives photos of food a natural appearance by using medium levels of contrast and color saturation. The symbol of this mode is a fork and knife.

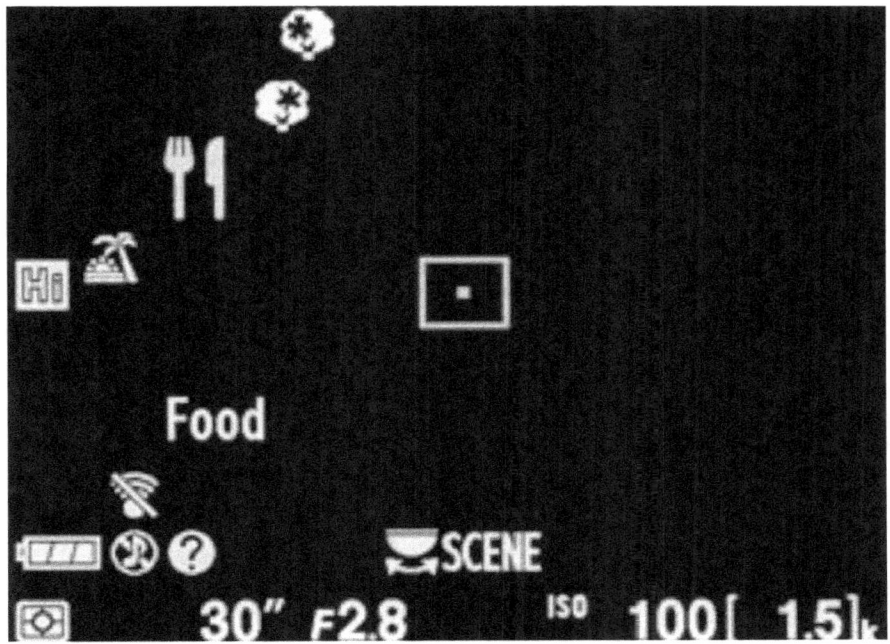

In order to get sufficient depth of field to concentrate the majority of the food that is being captured, this mode prioritizes smaller apertures. Note; if you are using this mode and taking pictures of food in dim light, use a tripod.

Scene Mode for Silhouettes

When you photograph a silhouette in this mode, the camera lights up the backdrop and then darkens the subject. Since the camera turns off the pop-up flash while using the silhouette scene mode, it is not recommended for capturing photos of people standing in front of windows; instead, use the portrait or night portrait scene modes. Recommendably, you take advantage of this mode to capture fascinating foreground objects, such as trees, in shadow against a

117

stunning sky or sunset. The symbol used to represent this mode is a palm tree and sunset.

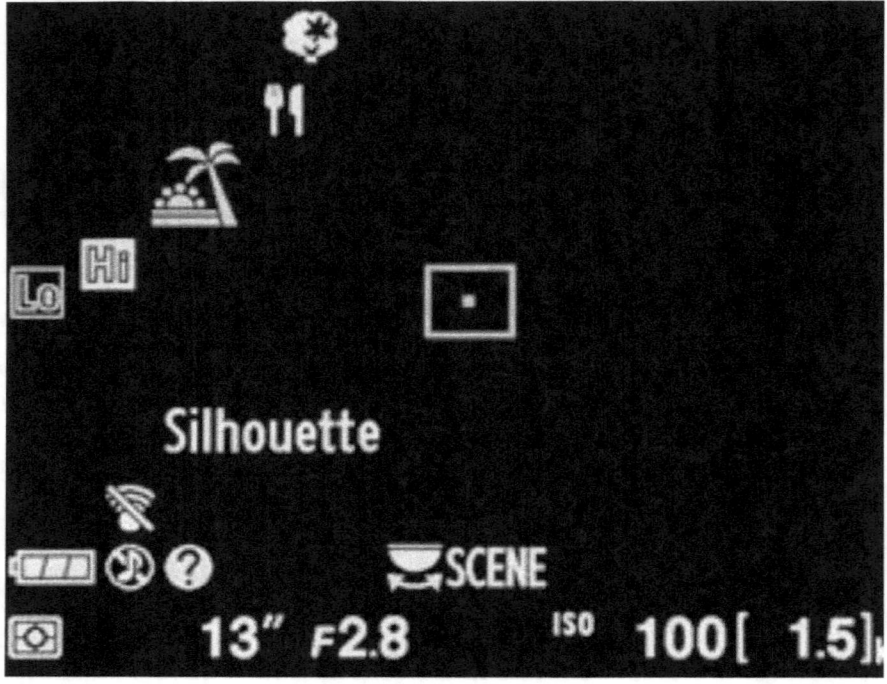

Note: While using this mode, once the focus is already set, the camera locks the subject.

High Key Scene Mode

To make the picture seem very brilliant, high-key photography is purposefully overexposed to some extent. It almost looks to be glowing more brightly than usual, erasing some of the highlight details of the mode. The word "hi" is the mode's icon.

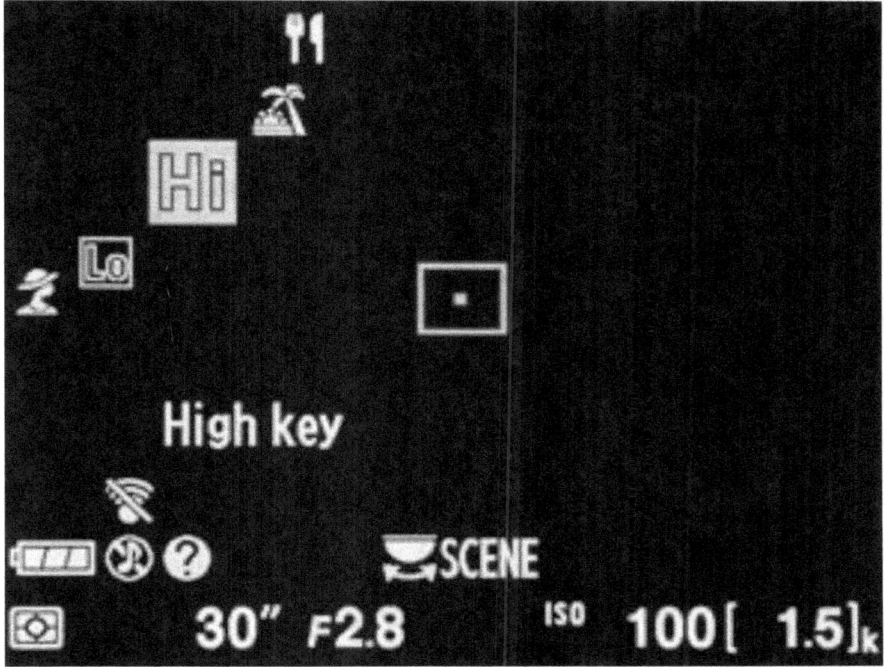

For a bright and dreamy look, if you want to shoot white subjects on white backgrounds, utilize the high key scene mode. In order to preserve certain highlights, the contrast is somewhat reduced, and the brightness is automatically increased. In this mode, the focus assist light and pop-up flash are disabled. Note: The camera locks focus on the subject, once it acquires the accurate focus.

Low Key Scene Mode

In low-key photography, the highlights are everything. The Low-key scene mode works nicely for reflections from sparkling subjects. The word "Lo" serves as the symbol for this mode.

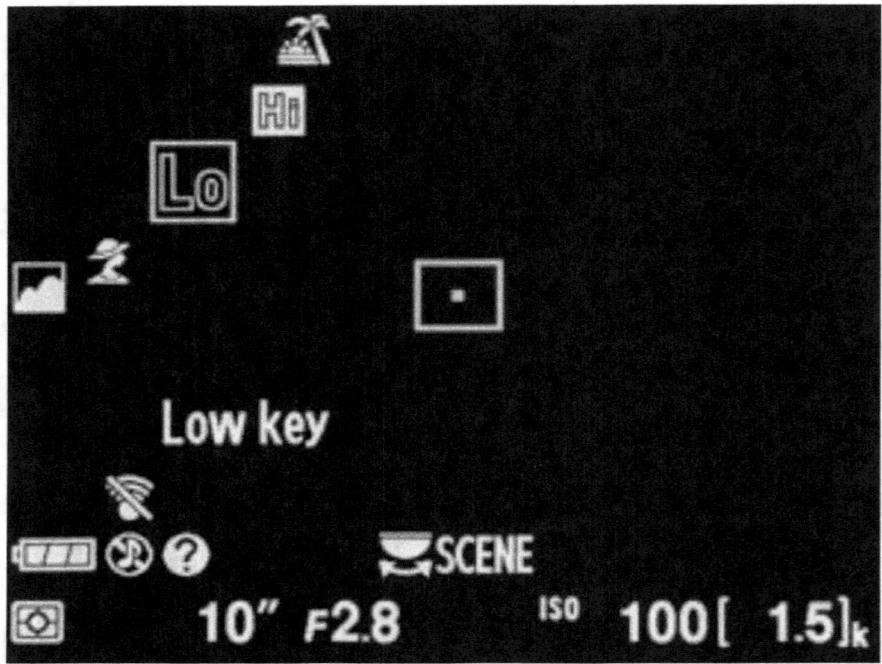

When you want to keep the highlights while keeping the majority of the subject appearing gloomy and melancholic, use the Low Key Scene setting. In order to accentuate the shadows, the camera automatically reduces brightness and increases contrast. When shooting in this mode, it's a good idea to use a tripod because of the low light. Given that gloomy photographs often do not highlight color, the color saturation is set to medium. In this mode, the focus assist light and pop-up flash are disabled. Note: The camera locks focus on the subject once it acquires the accurate focus.

How to Understand the Histogram

By employing the camera histogram scenes, one can ensure a significantly greater proportion of images with proper exposure. It is therefore highly beneficial to invest effort in comprehending the histogram.

Light Range

Firstly, note that the maximum range of light value which the camera can record is a ten or eleven EV steps. Further note that understanding the light recording mechanism of the camera is crucial in order to exert greater control over your captured image.

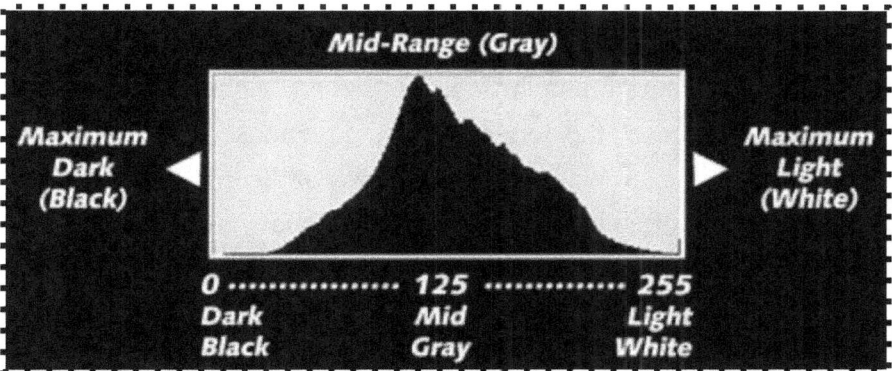

In 256 stages, the histogram illustrates the broadest possible spectrum of light values that a camera is capable of capturing (from 0 to 255, where 0 represents pure black and 255 represents pure white). The values in the midrange of the histogram correspond to colors in the middle to the spectrum, such as mild browns, grays, and greens. The histogram graph resembles a mountain peak or a succession of peaks;

in an RGB histogram, the height of the peak for a specific color increases if that specific color is in abundance. Occasionally the upper portion of the graph will be rounded, while at other times it will be flat.

The histogram illustrates the maximum dark values that can be captured by the camera on the left side, and the maximum light values on the right side. If the light values at both extremes of the histogram lack any discernible information, then they are entirely white or entirely black in color.

An individual color is represented by the peak height of the histogram, which resembles the top of mountains. Changing to a Picture Control with a more or less saturated color is the only way to readily adjust this value in-camera; therefore, it is provided for your information only. Since we possess considerably more authority over obscurity and light, the values on the histogram's left and right are primarily of interest. In essence, the left and right directions of the histogram correspond to the luminance and luminosity of the image, whereas the up and down directions (represented by the valleys and peaks) represent the quantity of color information (i.e., the number of pixels assigned to each color). When photographing, the left (dark) and right (light) directions are crucial. The histogram will indicate whether the image is excessively dark or light by cropping the light values on the left and right, respectively.

Note; a significantly blank area will appear on the right side of the histogram window when the image is underexposed and is reflected to the left of the window and cropped mid peak. Additionally, the boundaries of the well-exposed histogram will intersect with the left and right margins of the histogram window when an image is properly exposed. Furthermore, in the case of an overexposed image, the histogram representing the overexposure will be cropped to the right.

How the Histogram Shape Looks Like and What They Represent.

Your image is perfectly exposed when the entire light spectrum is contained within the histogram window. This indicates that the image is neither overly bright nor black, and minimal or no adjustments are required. Be aware, however, that for an exposure to be satisfactory, a histogram need not encompass the entire aperture. This is because the histogram may be relatively constrained in the presence of a very restricted spectrum of light.

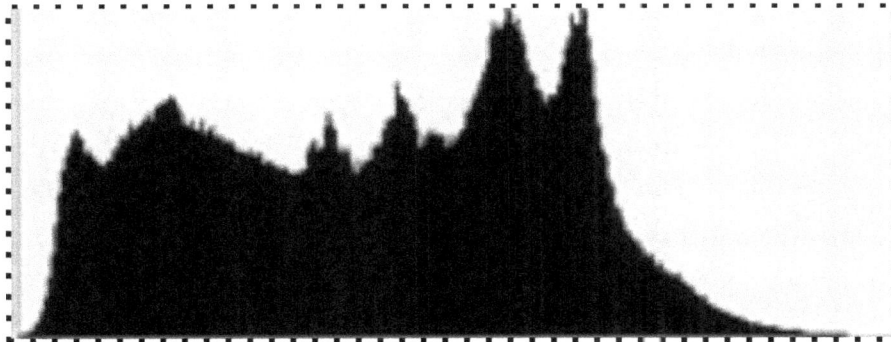

Further, a mountain-shaped histogram is a reflection of an image that is relatively subdued and has seamless tonal transitions. However, this shape does not manifest itself consistently, as images comprise a substantial amount of color information variation, as indicated by the peaks. A distinct apex will be assigned to each conspicuous color in an RGB histogram. Colors that are less prominent will have lesser or no peaks, while those that are most prominent will have higher peaks. However, this occurs when the dim values of an image surpass the sensor's range. The histogram is truncated and compressed to the left. In contrast to a mountain range, which consists of gradual ascents from valley to peak and then back to valley, there are no such gradual climbs. Conversely, the image appears in mid peak on the left side.

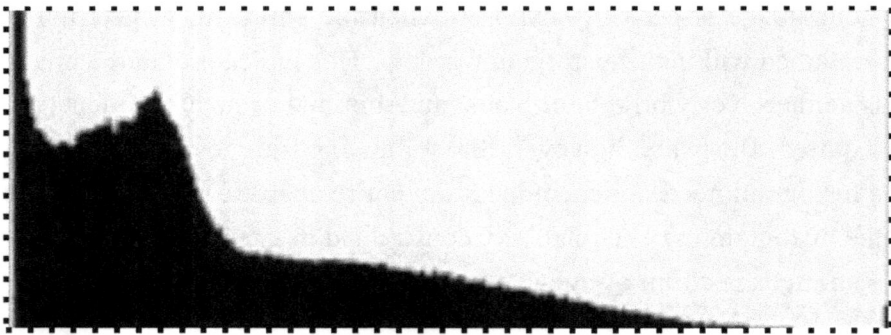

It should be noted that the presence of a truncated portion of the peak on the left side of a histogram indicates that either a portion or the entirety of the image is considerably underexposed. Additionally, keep in mind that when a larger aperture is employed and more light is permitted in an image, the highlight side (right) and dark side (left) of the histogram will be cropped.

A histogram that is extremely skewed to the right and left indicates that both the light and dark regions of the image have significantly diminished in detail. To counteract this, however, attempt to center the histogram so that neither margin is clipped.

By centering the histogram, the exposure of your images will be improved. In situations where the histogram cannot be centered due to excessive light, one must determine the relative importance of the bright and dark regions of the image and adjust the exposure accordingly.

Luminance Differences in the Histogram

In a sense, the luminance histogram is a combination of the histograms of the three RGB channels.

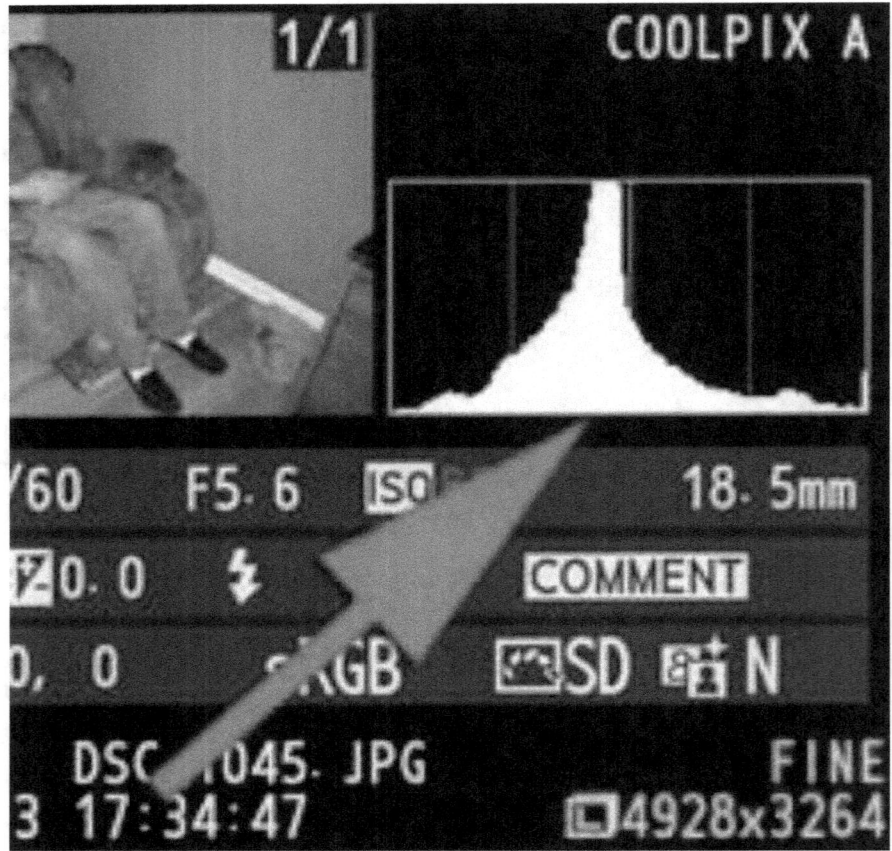

It is not, nevertheless, a precise combination. It is a combination of weighted luminosity. Additionally, the predominant color in nature is green, which significantly influences human visual perception. The luminosity of a luminance histogram is therefore weighted as follows: Thirty-one percent red, five-nine percent blue.

Using the luminance histogram will yield the most accurate results in most cases. The sole purpose for which the majority of individuals require access to the histogram of a single color channel (RGB) is to determine whether or not a particularly vivid hue, like red, has completely obscured all detail in that channel.

Does the Histogram Represents a JPEG Image?

The camera processes RAW image information from the sensor prior to capturing an image. It then compresses the 14 bits of color information into an 8-bit space, thereby discarding any excess color information. Given that subtle variations in brightness are considerably more perceptible to the human eye than subtle variations in color, the elimination of six bits of color information does not significantly impact the image quality, provided that the brightness remains unaffected.

On the contrary, a RAW image captured by a Nikon camera typically has a slight advantage over a JPEG due to its greater color information. In other words, in the event that a histogram exhibits clipping on the light or dark sides, the clipping is a result of the JPEG compression that the camera generates. Darker and brighter regions of the image would contain slightly more detail than what is displayed on the histogram if the image were captured in NEF (RAW) mode.

However, there have been compelling arguments in favor of capturing high-contrast scenes in RAW format. This is due to the fact that in RAW mode, your images will experience less detail loss in both bright and dark regions. However, if you are photographing in RAW mode, the histogram's representation of the scene acquired by the camera is slightly conservative. But Note: The histogram will be precise if you only capture JPEGs.

How Does White Balance Work?

White balance is typically employed to calibrate the camera in order to ensure that all colors are accurate and whites appear as intended, regardless of the light source that is present during the photographing process. For intriguing special effects, you can also intentionally incorporate color casts into your images using the white balance controls.

Color Temperature

The WB range of the camera can be adjusted from an extremely cold 2700K to an extremely balmy 8000K.

When shooting in direct sunlight, to obtain the same effect as using a warming filter and daylight film, simply select the Cloudy white balance setting. This adjusts the camera's balance to approximately 6000K, producing images with a pleasant warmth. To significantly intensify the image, select "Shade" which is a white balance setting and adjusts the camera's temperature to 8000K. Alternatively, the white balance could be adjusted to Auto2 by navigating to Shooting Menu > White Balance > Auto, which would intensify the colors and adjust automatically for available light sources.

Conversely, to achieve a bluish or cold appearance for the image during natural light, experiment with the Fluorescent (4200K) or Incandescent (3000K) settings.

Bear in mind that as the color temperature increases, it transitions from cold to mild. The camera is capable of capturing images at a wide range of color temperatures, including 2700K (extremely cold or bluish), 8000K (extremely heated or ruddy), and several significant values in between. The camera's color temperature effect eliminates the necessity to transport various film emulsions or filters in order to capture a spectrum of light colors. This is due to the camera's comprehensive color temperature range and user-friendly color temperature controls. If you wish to apply tints to your photographs, the following is a list of the WB settings and color temperatures on the camera:

Kelvin value	White balance option
2700K	Fluorescent (Sodium-vapor lamps)
3000K	Incandescent
3000K	Fluorescent (Warm-white)
3700K	Fluorescent (White)
4200K	Fluorescent (Cool-white)
5000K	Fluorescent (Day-white)
5200K	Direct sunlight
5400K	Flash
6000K	Cloudy
6500K	Fluorescent (Daylight)
7200K	Fluorescent (High temp. mercury-vapor)
8000K	Shade

Going further, there are symbols which denote the White balance settings in the Quick Menu and the Shooting Menu, and the symbols are located beneath the White balance setting. The symbols, names, and Kelvin WB values are as follows:

Kelvin value	Symbol	White balance option
3500K–8000K	AUTO1/AUTO2	Auto WB
3000K	☀	Incandescent
2700K–7200K	▦	Fluorescent
5200K	☀	Direct sunlight
5400K	⚡	Flash
6000K	☁	Cloudy
8000K	⌂	Shade
Ambient reading	PRE	Preset manual

Manual White Balance Using the Shooting Menu

The Shooting Menu option provides the settings to manually adjust the white balance, enabling the user to choose their preferable Kelvin color temperature. You can also select a particular white balance value from the list of available values on the Shooting Menu Screen. Utilize the Shooting Menu to configure, fine-tune, and choose a WB initially, as it provides a more extensive selection. Follow the procedures below, to select a white balance via the Shooting Menu.

1. Go to the Shooting Menu, and then scroll rightwards. After which you will see the white balance option, click on it to select.

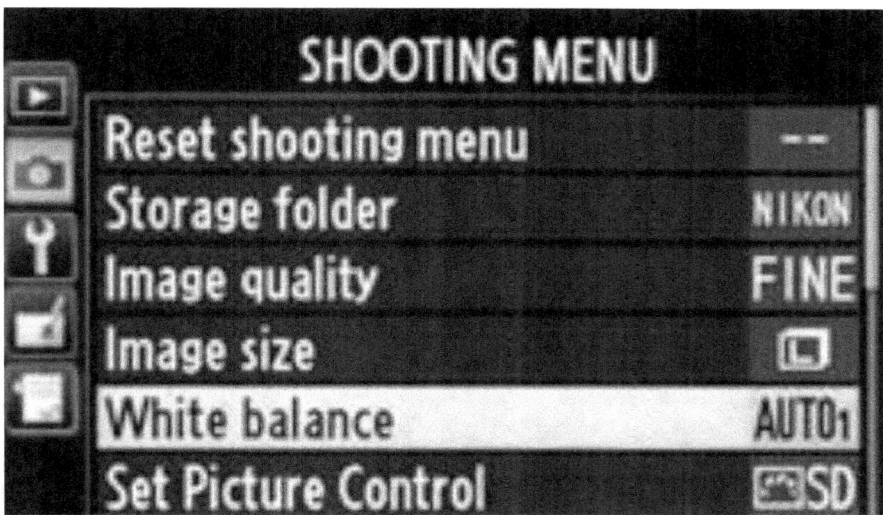

2. Scroll to the right and select one of the preset values, such as Cloudy or Flash.

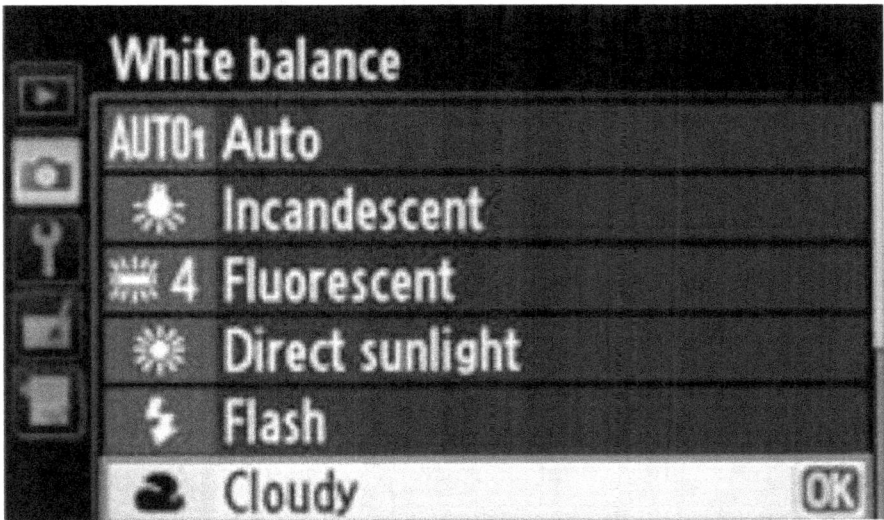

3. Immediately press the OK button while ensuring that the black square remains in its center position in the color box, unless you intend to adjust the white balance setting.

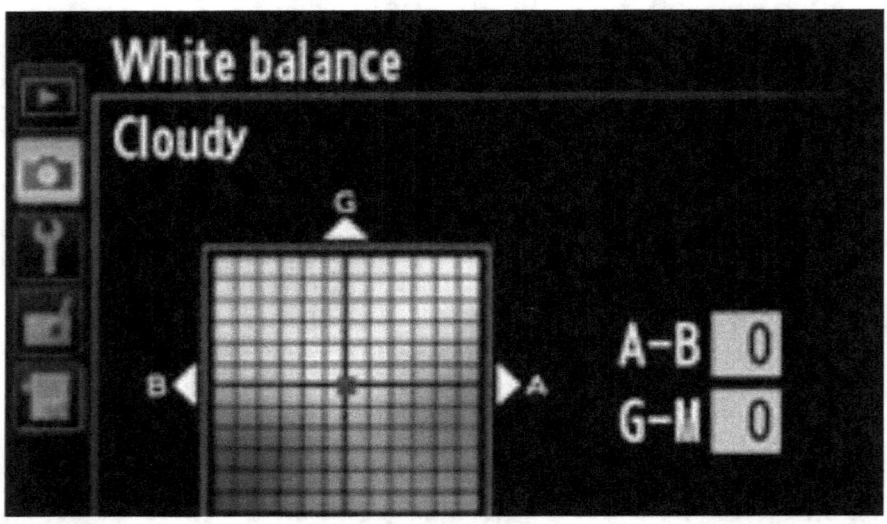

However, as stated previously, you are only permitted to choose one of the preset WB values, including Cloudy, Shade, or Direct sunlight. You will then click the OK icon without making any further changes on the final screen. However, after selecting one of the preset WB values in the color box, it is possible to fine-tune any of the color temperature parameters with a minimum of two clicks. But you must note; each rotation of the multi-selector in a specific direction corresponds to five mirror movements in that direction: green (G) indicates up, magenta (M) signifies down, blue (B) signifies left, and amber (A) signifies right. However, in the event that you lack experience or desire to remain uninformed regarding the modification of the preset default color temperature, merely click the OK button while keeping the black square in the middle of the color box. In the event of an inadvertent relocation of the black square, simply realign it with the center position using the Multi Selector and proceed by pressing the OK button. This will select the default value of the WB without modifying it.

It should be noted that the Fluorescent option provides access to a diverse range of seven distinct light sources, encompassing a broad spectrum of Kelvin values. Note; if you choose Fluorescent option, you will observe an additional screen that appears between the other screens when you are following the steps (as outlined above) to adjust the White Balance via the Shooting Menu Screen.

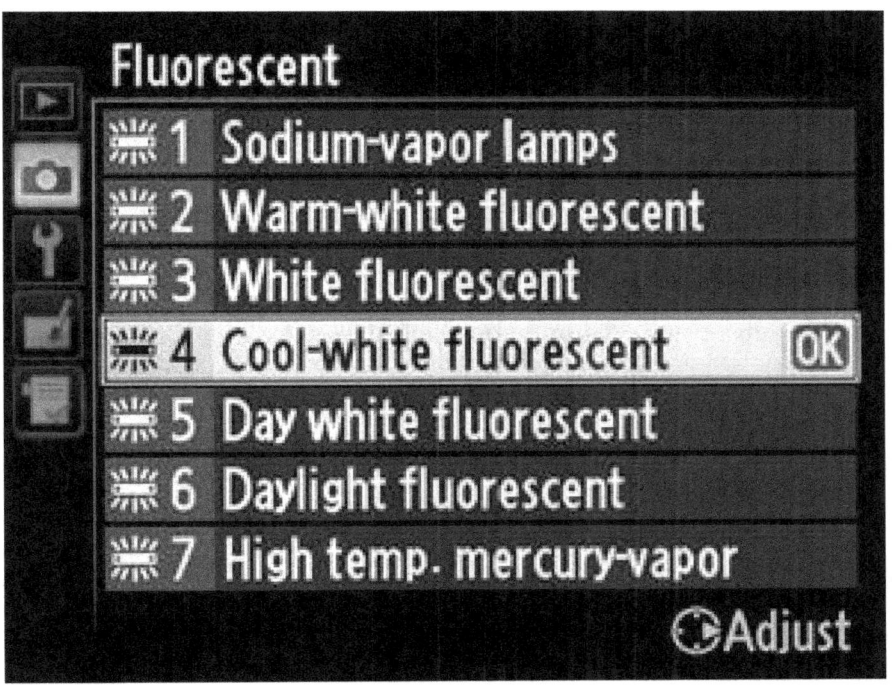

Note: While WB may not be as critical when capturing images that are unrelated to one another, it is still crucial that it accurately represents the colors of the subject. In essence, Auto WB performs admirably for the majority of common photography tasks. Nevertheless, in a production setting, such as a studio, where the white balance (WB) cannot be altered, it is critical to utilize one of the preset WB values that corresponds to the color temperature (e.g., flash or direct sunlight) required for consistent shots.

White Balance Selection via the Quick Menu

White balance values are accessible via the Shooting Menu as well as the Quick Menu. Following our previous discussion on the Shooting Menu method, we shall now provide a concise overview of the Quick Menu method. The Quick Menu does not permit adjustments, including fine-tuning, nor does it permit selection of individual fluorescent options, which is possible from the Shooting Menu. Follow the procedures below to select a preset WB value in the Quick Menu:

1. Tap on the i Button and click on Quick Menu as soon as it appears, select White balance (WB). Press the OK button to access a selection of WB values.

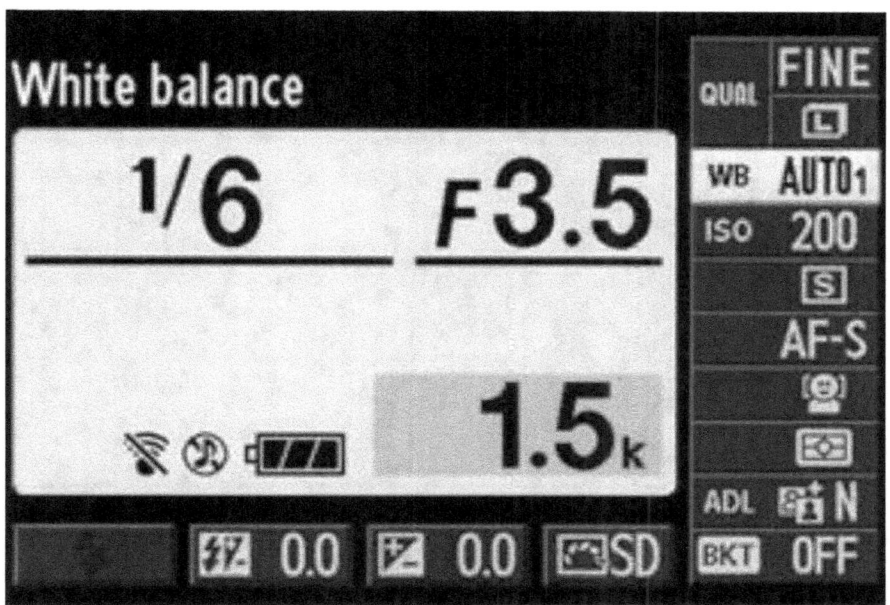

2. Choose from the available preset options, including Auto1, Flash, or Cloudy.

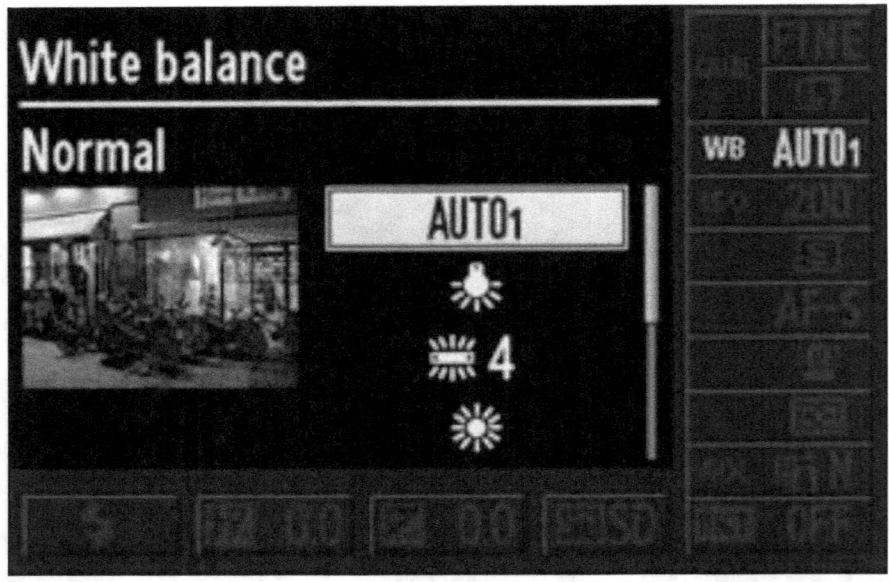

3. Click the OK button to activate that WB value which you have chosen.

Note; the Quick Menu only allows you to select a single fluorescent valu, which is the one you previously selected in the Shooting Menu > White balance setting. Additionally, the previous PRE reading (ambient light reading) is an option that can be selected by you, and it is the last option in the White balance menu. The PRE option can also be selected through the manual process of analyzing reflected light from a white or gray card via the Shooting Menu > White balance > Preset method.

Auto White Balance

Automatic white balance in the camera functions adequately. The camera endeavors to achieve color balance by detecting and adjusting for any white or midrange grays present in the image. However, each picture will have a slight variation in color. When shooting exclusively in Auto WB mode, the camera processes each image as an individual WB problem and resolves it independently of the most recent image captured. As a result, when utilizing Auto WB, the color balance of each individual image might vary slightly.

There are two varieties of automatic white balance: Auto1 and Auto2. Auto2 employs hues that are richer in tone than Auto1. The procedure for choosing one of the Auto White balance options is as follows:

1. From the Shooting Menu, select White balance and navigate to the right.

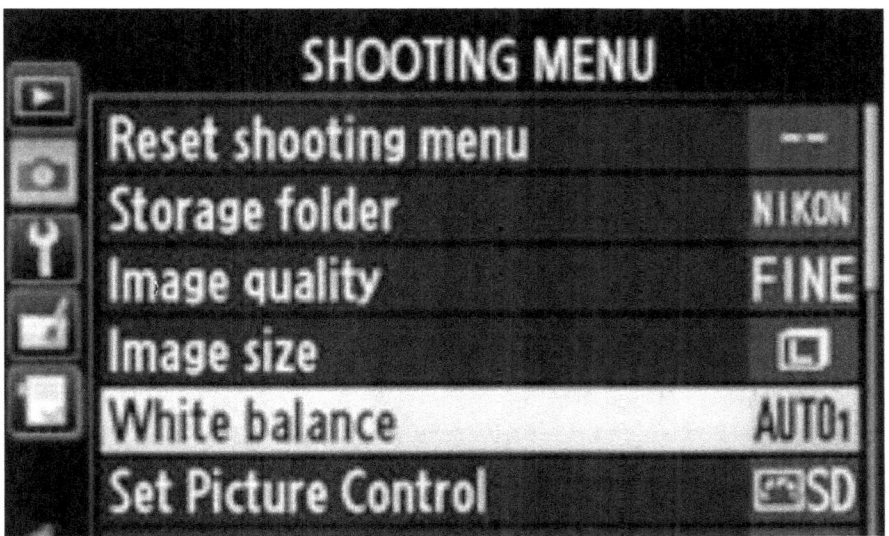

2. Click on the Auto options and navigate rightwards.

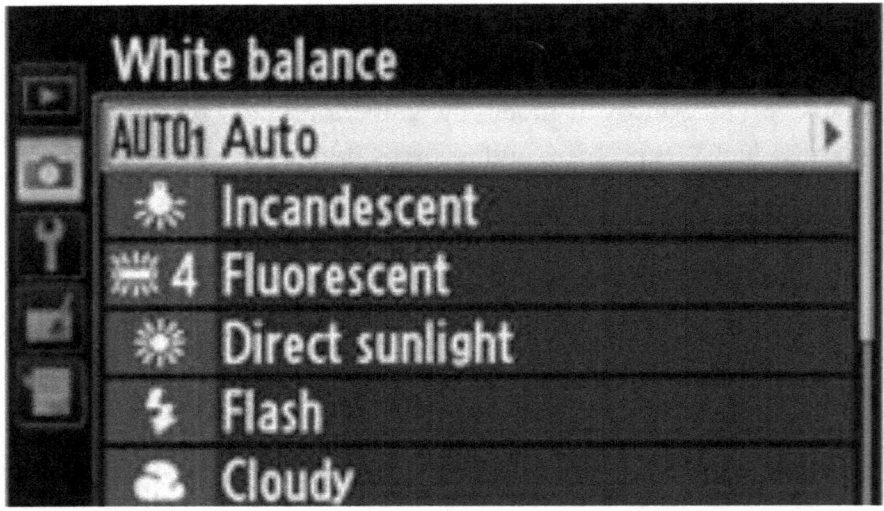

3. Select Auto 2 or Auto1, in accordance with your preferred color temperature.

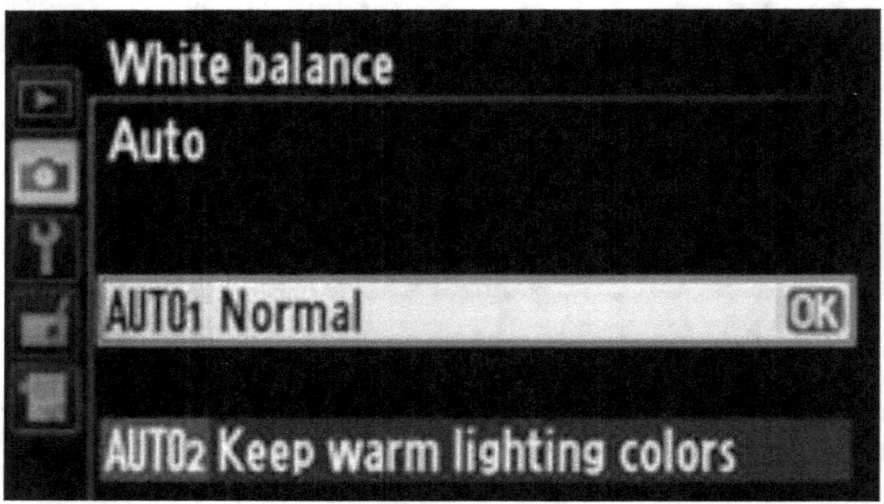

If you are not interested in fine-tuning the white balance setting, proceed to the subsequent step without scrolling to the right.

4. To lock in the WB setting, press the OK button.

It is possible to utilize the Auto1 white balance at any circumstance. You can only refrain from using it when capturing unique varieties of images. For example, when photographing an event using a light and desiring consistent coloration throughout the image, the white balance can be adjusted to light rather than Auto White Balance. Additionally, when photographing landscapes in direct sunlight, the Direct sunlight white balance setting can be utilized rather than the Auto White Balance setting. Other than that, Auto white balance performs admirably.

Applying the WB from an Image Captured Previously

Additionally, a white balance setting can be extracted from a previously captured image. Here are the procedures for retrieving the white balance setting from a memory card containing an image that you are about to capture using the WB value from the previous screenshot.

1. Select White Balance from the Shooting Menu and navigate rightwards.

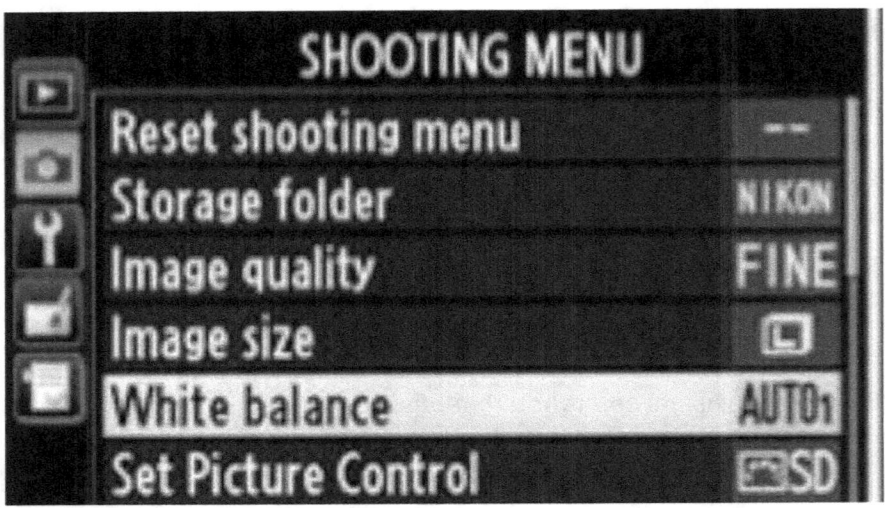

2. Browse through the selections and select the PRE Preset manual option.

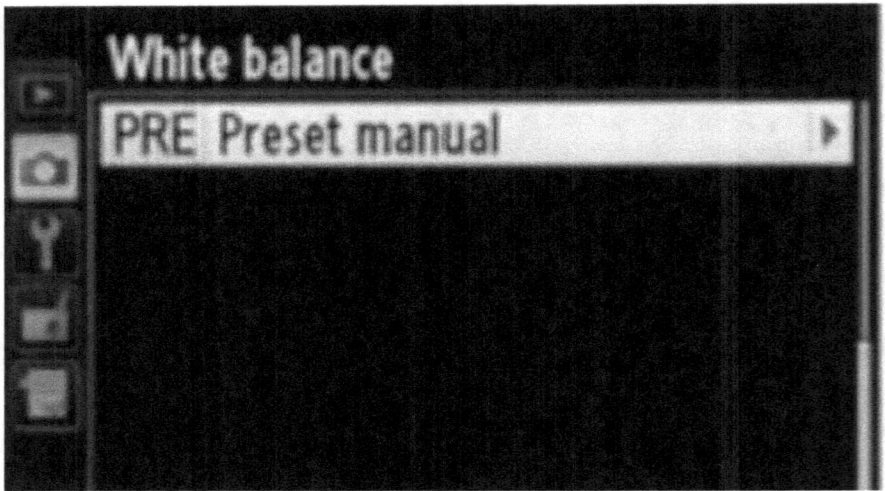

3. Tap the Use Photo settings and then browse rightwards

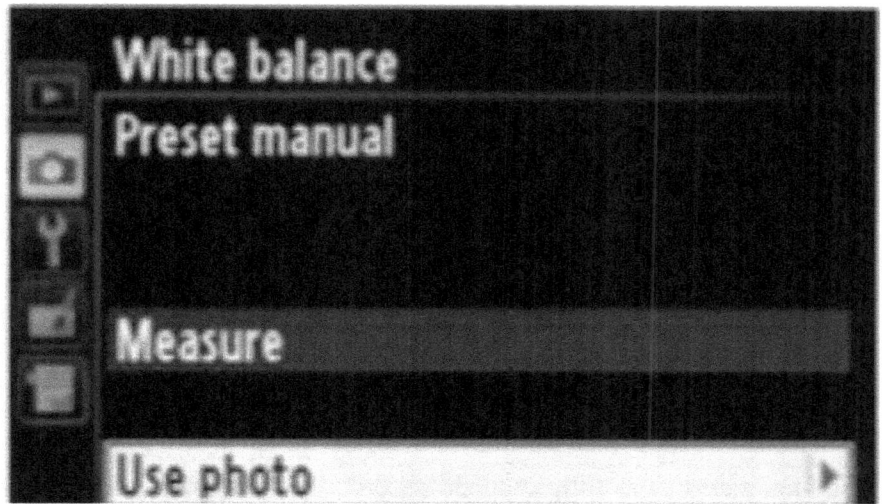

4. If these steps have been completed previously, the image that was utilized will be displayed. To reuse it, select the This Image Option and skip the subsequent two steps. In the absence of prior use of this function, a white rectangle resembling a thumbnail will be displayed in place of the thumbnail image. Conversely, if you wish to utilize an alternative image as the source of the WB, click on Select image and proceed to the right.

5. There will be a selection of folders containing images displayed. After identifying a folder, navigate to the right.

6. You will be presented with six thumbnail images; however, by rotating the Multi Selector Dial, you can navigate through all the images in the folder. Select the image captured using the desired WB and click the OK button. At this point, the camera would have adjusted the WB value. A screen

containing a thumbnail of the newly selected image will appear. Finally, complete the procedure by clicking the OK icon.

Fine Tuning the White Balance

With the Shooting Menu WB options, it is possible to adjust the white balance to produce a greater amount of a specific color. The Set function can be utilized to refine a White balance value that has been previously stored. It is possible to explicitly modify the value stored in memory locations d-0 through d-4. One has the ability to adjust the color balance in the following directions: toward green (G), amber (A), magenta (M), or blue (B), or toward intermediate color combinations thereof. To refine a white balance setting through the Shooting Menu options, follow these instructions:

1. From the Shooting Menu, select White balance and then navigate to the right.

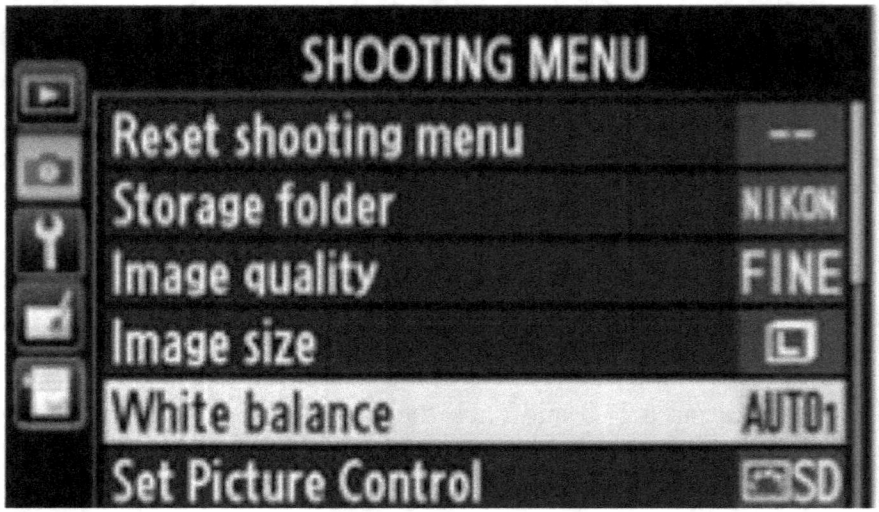

2. Select an option for the white balance from the menu.

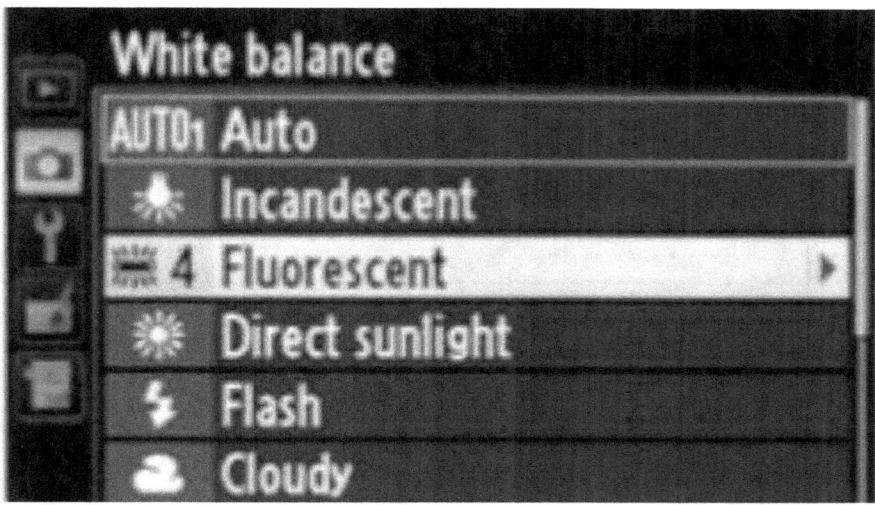

After selecting an option, proceed by browsing rightwards

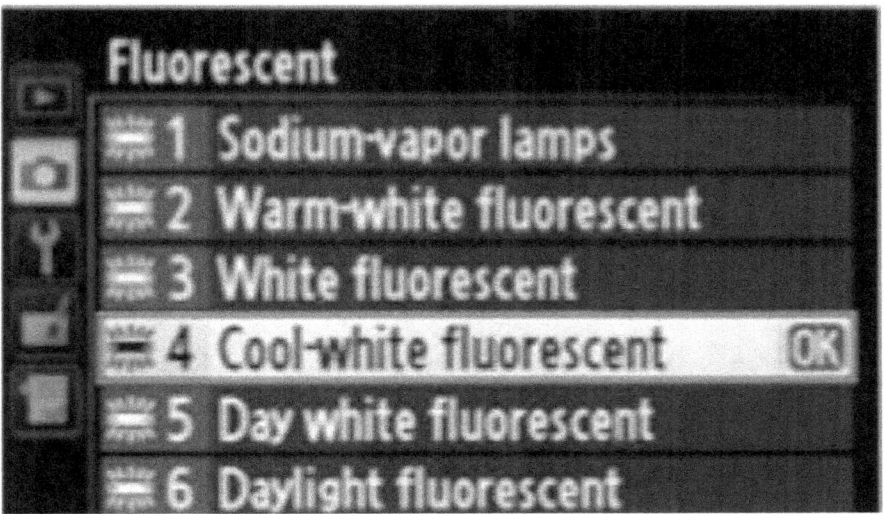

3.   To modify the color balance, rotate the Multi Selector to drag the black square positioned in the center of the color box in any direction.

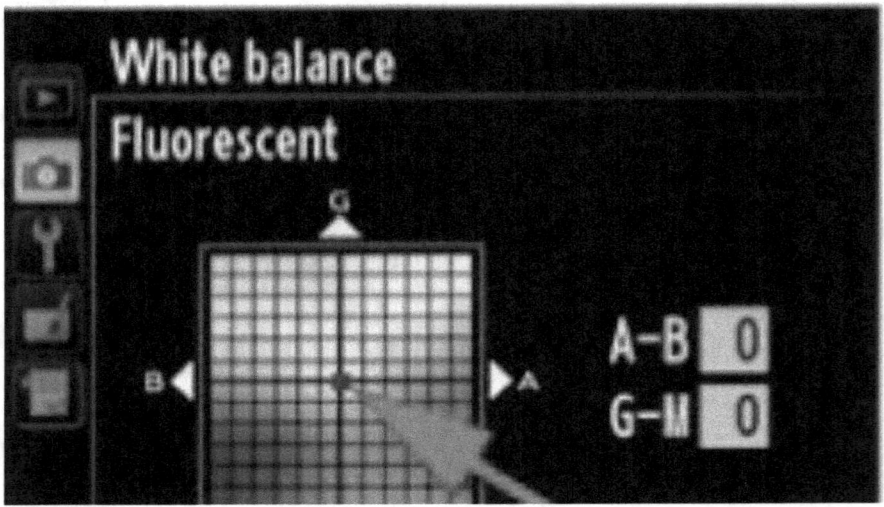

However, if you choose not to fine tune the White Balance subsequently, reposition the black square to the color box's center. The modified values will be displayed on the right, adjacent to A–B and G–M. Five-and-a-half mirror steps comprise each increment (click) of the Multi Selector Dial. Therefore, setting A–B to A3 results in the addition of 15-mired of amber to the existing WB; conversely, setting G–M to G3 signifies the addition of 15-mired of green to the existing WB.

4.   To save the modification made to the present White balance option which you have chosen, click the OK icon.

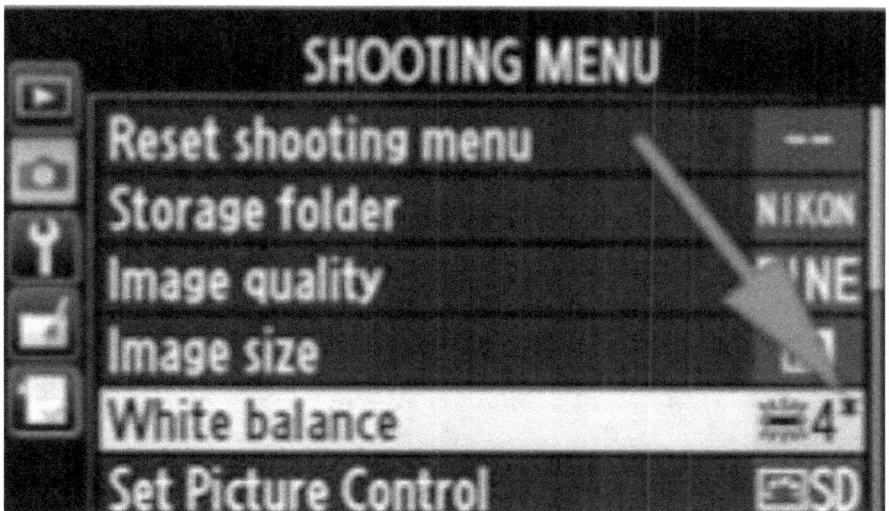

Note: An additional indication that the WB option has been modified is the presence of a small asterisk sign next to it. Position the black square in the center of the color box and select the OK button in order to revert the WB option back to its initial setting. Thereafter, the asterisk sign will vanish.